First World War
and Army of Occupation
War Diary
France, Belgium and Germany

24 DIVISION
Divisional Troops
108 Brigade Royal Field Artillery
28 August 1915 - 28 December 1916

WO95/2197/5

The Naval & Military Press Ltd
www.nmarchive.com
Published in association with The National Archives

Published by

The Naval & Military Press Ltd

Unit 10 Ridgewood Industrial Park,

Uckfield, East Sussex,

TN22 5QE England

Tel: +44 (0) 1825 749494

www.naval-military-press.com

www.nmarchive.com

This diary has been reprinted in facsimile from the original. Any imperfections are inevitably reproduced and the quality may fall short of modern type and cartographic standards.

© Crown Copyright
Images reproduced by permission of The National Archives, London, England, 2015.

Contents

Document type	Place/Title	Date From	Date To
Heading	WO95/2197-5		
Heading	108th Brigade R.F.A. Sep 1915-Dec 1916		
Heading	Headquarters 108th Brigade, R.F.A. (24th Division) September (28.8.15 to 30.9.15) 1915		
War Diary	Deepcut.	28/08/1915	31/08/1915
War Diary	Havre	01/09/1915	01/09/1915
War Diary	Marles	03/09/1915	09/09/1915
War Diary	Laires	10/09/1915	11/09/1915
War Diary	Aire.	11/09/1915	11/09/1915
War Diary	Haverskerque	12/09/1915	12/09/1915
War Diary	Bout-Deville	13/09/1915	17/09/1915
War Diary	Grenay	18/09/1915	25/09/1915
War Diary	Le Routoir	26/09/1915	28/09/1915
War Diary	Noyelles	29/09/1915	30/09/1915
War Diary	Appendices 108/1 to 109/1.		
Miscellaneous	A Form. Messages And Signals.	09/09/1915	09/09/1915
Miscellaneous	A Form. Messages And Signals.		
Miscellaneous	A Form. Messages And Signals.	17/09/1915	17/09/1915
Miscellaneous	7th Brigade	11/09/1915	11/09/1915
Miscellaneous	7th Brigade R H A		
Miscellaneous	7th Bde. R.H.A.	11/09/1915	11/09/1915
Miscellaneous	7th Brigade R.H.A.	13/09/1915	13/09/1915
Miscellaneous	Headquarters, 7th Bde. R.H.A.	12/09/1915	12/09/1915
Miscellaneous	Arrangements For Gun Ammunition Supply.	11/09/1915	11/09/1915
Map			
Miscellaneous	108 Bde R.F.A.	24/09/1915	24/09/1915
Miscellaneous	A Form. Messages And Signals.	26/09/1915	26/09/1915
Miscellaneous	A Form. Messages And Signals.		
Miscellaneous	A Form. Messages And Signals.	26/09/1915	26/09/1915
Miscellaneous		26/09/1915	26/09/1915
Miscellaneous	Code G D R 48		
Miscellaneous	Left Group Operation Order no I		
Miscellaneous			
Miscellaneous	A Form. Messages And Signals.	27/09/1915	27/09/1915
Miscellaneous	Brigade Orders.		
Miscellaneous	Orders by Col. H.T. Butcher. R.F.A. No. 2	05/09/1915	05/09/1915
Miscellaneous	Orders by Col. H.T. Butcher. R.F.A. No. 3	06/09/1915	06/09/1915
Miscellaneous	Orders By Col. H.T. Butcher. R.F.A. No. 4	07/09/1915	07/09/1915
Miscellaneous	Orders by Col. H.T. Butcher. R.F.A. No. 5	08/09/1915	08/09/1915
Miscellaneous	Orders by Col. H.T. Butcher. R.F.A. No. 6	09/09/1915	09/09/1915
Miscellaneous	Orders by Col. H.T. Butcher. R.F.A. No. 7	10/09/1915	10/09/1915
Miscellaneous	Orders by Col. H.T. Butcher. R.F.A. No. 8	11/09/1915	11/09/1915
Miscellaneous	Orders by Col. H.T. Butcher. R.F.A. No. 9	12/09/1915	12/09/1915
Miscellaneous	108th Brigade Orders.	04/09/1915	04/09/1915
Miscellaneous	Orders by Col. H.T. Butcher. R.F.A. No. 10	13/09/1915	13/09/1915
Miscellaneous	Orders by Col. H.T. Butcher. R.F.A. No. 11	16/09/1915	16/09/1915
Miscellaneous	Orders by Col. H.T. Butcher. R.F.A. No. 12	17/09/1915	17/09/1915
Miscellaneous	108th Brigade Orders by Major the Hon. R. Hamilton. R.F.A. No. 18	22/09/1915	22/09/1915
Miscellaneous	The O.C. A,B,C, & D Btys. HQ. 108th. Bde. R.F.A.		

Miscellaneous	108th Brigade Orders by Major the Hon. R. Hamilton. R.F.A. No. 19	13/09/1915	13/09/1915
Heading	24th Division 108th Bde: R.F.A. Vol 2 Oct 15		
War Diary	Noyelles	01/10/1915	03/10/1915
War Diary	Vieux Berquin	04/10/1915	04/10/1915
War Diary	Proven	05/10/1915	07/10/1915
War Diary	Boeschepe	08/10/1915	27/10/1915
Miscellaneous	A Form. Messages And Signals.		
Miscellaneous	A Form. Messages And Signals.	07/10/1915	07/10/1915
Miscellaneous	A Form. Messages And Signals.		
Miscellaneous	A Form. Messages And Signals.	03/10/1915	03/10/1915
Miscellaneous		01/10/1915	01/10/1915
Miscellaneous	Orders by Lt Col Cartwright DSO Comdg Left Grouh R.F.A.		
Miscellaneous	To O.C. 108th Bde	02/10/1915	02/10/1915
Miscellaneous	To O.C. 108th Brigade. R.F.A. From O.C. Left Grouh		
Miscellaneous	108th. Brigade Orders by Major the Hon. R. Hamilton. R.F.A. No. 20	03/10/1915	03/10/1915
Miscellaneous	108th. Brigade Orders by Major the Hon. R. Hamilton. R.F.A. No. 21	04/10/1915	04/10/1915
Miscellaneous	108th Brigade Orders by Lt. Col. E.C. Walthall. D.S.O., R.F.A.	05/10/1915	05/10/1915
Miscellaneous	108th. Brigade Orders by Bt. Lt. Col. E.C. Walthall. D.S.O., R.F.A. No. 23.	06/10/1915	06/10/1915
Miscellaneous	108th. Brigade Orders by Bt. Lt. Col. E.C. Walthall. R.F.A. No. 24.	07/10/1915	07/10/1915
Miscellaneous	108th. Brigade Orders by Lt. Col. E.C. Walthall. D.S.O., R.F.A.	08/10/1916	08/10/1916
Operation(al) Order(s)	108th. Brigade Orders by Bt. Lt. Col. E.C. Walthall. D.S.O., R.F.A. No.26.	09/10/1915	09/10/1915
Operation(al) Order(s)	108th. Brigade Orders by Lt. Col. E.C. Walthall. D.S.O. R.F.A. No. 27.	10/10/1915	10/10/1915
Operation(al) Order(s)	108th. Brigade Orders. by Bt. Lt. Col. E.C. Walthall. D.S.O., R.F.A. No. 28.	11/10/1915	11/10/1915
Operation(al) Order(s)	108th. Brigade Orders. by Bt. Lt. Col. E.C. Walthall. D.S.O. R.F.A. No. 29	12/10/1915	12/10/1915
Miscellaneous	108th. Brigade Orders by Bt. Lt. Col. E.C. Walthall. D.S.O., R.F.A. No. 80	13/10/1915	13/10/1915
Operation(al) Order(s)	108th. Brigade Orders by Bt. Lt. Col. E.C. Walthall. D.S.O., R.F.A. No. 31	14/10/1915	14/10/1915
Operation(al) Order(s)	108th. Brigade Orders by Bt. Lt. Col. E.C. Walthall. D.S.O., R.F.A. No. 82	15/10/1915	15/10/1915
Operation(al) Order(s)	108th. Brigade R.F.A. by Bt. Lt. Col. E.C. Walthall. D.S.O., R.F.A. No. 88	16/10/1915	16/10/1915
Operation(al) Order(s)	108th. Brigade Orders by Bt. Lt. Col. E.C. Walthall. D.S.O., R.F.A. No. 34	17/10/1915	17/10/1915
Operation(al) Order(s)	108th. Brigade Orders by Bt. Lt. Col. E.C. Walthall. D.S.O. R.F.A. No. 35	18/10/1915	18/10/1915
Operation(al) Order(s)	108th. Brigade Orders by Bt. Lt. Col. E.C. Walthall. D.S.O., R.F.A. No. 36	19/10/1915	19/10/1915
Operation(al) Order(s)	108th. Brigade Orders by Bt. Lt. Col. E.C. Walthall. D.S.O., R.F.A. No. 37	21/10/1915	21/10/1915
Operation(al) Order(s)	108th. Brigade Orders by Bt. Lt. Col. E.C. Walthall. D.S.O., R.F.A. No. 38.	23/10/1915	23/10/1915
Operation(al) Order(s)	108th. Brigade Orders by Bt. Lt. Col. E.C. Walthall. D.S.O., R.F.A. No. 39.	26/10/1915	26/10/1915

Type	Description	From	To
Miscellaneous	108th. Brigade Orders by Bt. Lt. Col. E.C. Walthall. D.S.O., R.F.A. No. 40.	30/10/1915	30/10/1915
Operation(al) Order(s)	108th. Brigade Orders by Bt. Lt. Col. E.C. Walthall. D.S.O., R.F.A. No. 41	31/10/1915	31/10/1915
Heading	108 RFA Vol 7		
Heading	108th Bde RFA Vol 6		
Heading	24th Division 108th Bde R.7.a Vol 3 Nov. 15		
War Diary	Boeschepe	01/11/1915	04/11/1915
War Diary	Dickebusch	05/11/1915	24/11/1915
War Diary	Steenworde	25/11/1915	25/11/1915
War Diary	Aneke	27/11/1915	27/11/1915
War Diary	Moringhem	28/11/1915	30/11/1915
Heading	108 R.F.A. 24th Div Vol 4		
War Diary	Moringhem	01/12/1915	02/12/1915
War Diary	AL Quines	03/12/1915	31/12/1915
Heading	108th Bde. R.F.A. Vol 5 Jan '16		
War Diary	Alquines	01/01/1916	05/01/1916
War Diary	Quelmes	06/01/1916	08/01/1916
War Diary	Noordpeene	09/01/1916	09/01/1916
War Diary	Steenworde	10/01/1916	11/01/1916
War Diary	Zillebeke Lake	15/01/1916	19/01/1916
War Diary	Zillebeke	22/01/1916	31/01/1916
War Diary	Poperinghe	01/02/1916	16/02/1916
War Diary	Ypres	23/02/1916	04/03/1916
War Diary	Poperinghe	10/03/1916	10/03/1916
War Diary	Ypres	14/03/1916	15/03/1916
War Diary	Poperinghe	16/03/1916	18/03/1916
War Diary	Eecke	19/03/1916	01/04/1916
War Diary	Dranoutre	05/04/1916	23/07/1916
War Diary	Eecke	23/07/1916	26/07/1916
War Diary	Crouy	29/07/1916	31/07/1916
Heading	108th Brigade Royal Field Artillery August 1916		
War Diary	Daours	04/08/1916	04/08/1916
War Diary	Bois-Des-Tailles	11/08/1916	11/08/1916
War Diary	A2 d. 7 1/2. 6 1/2 (62.C)	12/08/1916	27/08/1916
Heading	108th Brigade R.F.A. September 1916		
War Diary	Sheet 62c. A2d.71/2 61/2	01/09/1916	06/09/1916
War Diary	Bois des Tailles	08/09/1916	11/09/1916
War Diary	F.23 b.	12/09/1916	14/09/1916
War Diary	S 30 b 1.3.	15/09/1916	21/09/1916
War Diary	T.25 a. 7.9 1/2	22/09/1916	28/09/1916
War Diary	Bois Des Tailles	29/09/1916	29/09/1916
War Diary	Talmas Sheet 11 Lens	30/10/1916	30/10/1916
Heading	Nominal Roll of Officers of 108th. Brigade R.F.A. by Batteries.		
War Diary	Bretel	01/10/1916	01/10/1916
War Diary	Blangermont	02/10/1916	02/10/1916
War Diary	Camblain & Chatelain	03/10/1916	03/10/1916
War Diary	Verdrel	04/10/1916	04/10/1916
War Diary	X.7.d.1.1.	07/10/1916	23/10/1916
War Diary	Villers Au Bois	23/10/1916	04/12/1916
War Diary	Noeux Les. Mines	04/12/1916	05/12/1916
War Diary	Les. Brebis	06/12/1916	28/12/1916

woof/2/9/5 spoon

24TH DIVISION
DIVL ARTILLERY

108TH BRIGADE R.F.A.
SEP 1915 - DEC 1916

To 4 ARMY

Brigade disembarked
Havre from England
1.9.15.

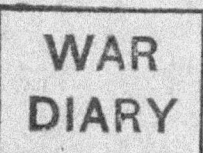
WAR DIARY

Headquarters,

108th BRIGADE, R.F.A.

(24th Division)

S E P T E M B E R

(28.8.15 to 30.9.15)

1 9 1 5

Dec '16

Attached:

Appendices 108/1
to 108/49.
Brigade Orders.

Army Form C. 2118

WAR DIARY
or
INTELLIGENCE SUMMARY.
(Erase heading not required.)

Headquarters
108th Bde. R.F.A.

Place	Date	Hour	Summary of Events and Information	Remarks and references to Appendices
	1915.			
DEEPCUT.	28.8.	—	Orders received to proceed overseas.	HAS
DEEPCUT.	31.8.	—	Brigade entrained at FARNBOROUGH commencing at 1.15 a.m. for SOUTHAMPTON. Left SOUTHAMPTON commencing 6 p.m. for HAVRE.	HAS
HAVRE.	1.9.	—	Arrived at HAVRE and disembarked at 7 a.m. Marched to Camp. Re S. Units commenced entraining at 8 p.m.	HAS
HAVRE.	2.9.	—	A/108, D/108 & 2499/108 entrained during the forenoon.	HAS
MARLES.	3.9.	—	Arrived at MONTREUIL at 4 a.m. and marched to MARLES where the Brigade went into billets.	HAS
MARLES.	4.9.	—	Remained in billets at MARLES.	HAS
MARLES.	5.9.	—	Remained in billets at MARLES.	HAS

Army Form C. 2118

WAR DIARY
or
INTELLIGENCE SUMMARY.
(Erase heading not required.)

Headquarters
108th Bde. R.F.A.

Place	Date	Hour	Summary of Events and Information	Remarks and references to Appendices
	1915.			
MARLES.	6.9.	—	Remained in Billets at MARLES.	HBrJ.
MARLES.	7.9.	—	The Brigade took part in a Divisional Exercise. Positions were taken up on the high ground N of LE DENOEUX. and then advanced to positions S.E. of ST OMER road 1 mile N.W. of SEMPY.	HBrJ.
MARLES.	8.9.	—	Nil.	HBrJ.
MARLES.	9.9.	—	Nil.	HBrJ.
LAIRES.	10.9.	—	Orders marked 108/1 (attached) were received at 9.40 p.m. last night. Brigade marched from MARLES at 8.30 a.m. and arrived at LAIRES at 5.30 p.m. Route:- ROYON-CREQUY -FRUGES. Billeted at LAIRES. Weather bright sunshine. Distance 24 miles. Condition of horses at end, good. S.A.A. Section of Bde A.C. left at MARLES under 2/Lt. Lewis. R.F.A.	HBrJ. 108/1.

Army Form C. 2118

WAR DIARY
INTELLIGENCE SUMMARY

Headquarters.
108th Bde. R.F.A.

(Erase heading not required.)

Instructions regarding War Diaries and Intelligence Summaries are contained in F.S. Regs., Part II and the Staff Manual respectively. Title pages will be prepared in manuscript.

Place	Date	Hour	Summary of Events and Information	Remarks and references to Appendices
	1915.		Map Hazebrouck 1.100.000.	
AIRE.	11.9.	6.15 p.m.	The Brigade marched to AIRE via ESTRÉE BLANCHE leaving LAIRES at 1.30 p.m. and arrived at 4 p.m. Distance 8 miles. Weather fine.	Appd.
HAVERSKERQUE	12.9.	9.30 a.m.	Marched to HAVERSKERQUE leaving AIRE at 10.15 a.m. Distance 8 miles. Weather fine.	Appd.
BOUT-DEVILLE	13.9.	—	Marched from HAVERSKERQUE at 10 a.m. Hq, A Bty & B Bty. marched to LAGORGUE and are attached to the MEERUT Division. C Bty, D Bty & Bde A.C. marched through MERVILLE to LABOUZATEUX Farm + are attached to the LAHORE Division. Hq. A + B Btys' wagon lines at cross-roads ¾ mile S of S in STA (near LA GORGUE) C + D Btys + Bde. A.C. wagon lines at LABOUZATEUX Farm. The Batteries went into action at 8 p.m. as follows. A + B Btys by Sections, A Bty 1 Sec. with the 14th Bty R.F.A. + B Bty 1 Sec. with the 44th Bty R.F.A. Positions A Bty near U in PONT DU HEM [P.T.O.]	Appd.

Army Form C. 2118.

WAR DIARY
INTELLIGENCE SUMMARY.

(Erase heading not required.)

Headquarters.
108th Bde. R.F.A.

Place	Date	Hour	Summary of Events and Information	Remarks and references to Appendices
BOUT DEVILLE.	1915. 13/9.		(continued) B Bty. ¼ mile N. of L in L'EPINETTE. C + D Btys. went in complete. Attached to Indian IV arty Group. Positions C Bty. at R in CROIX BARBEE & D Bty. at a point ¼ mile S of R in PONT DU HEM. Weather fine. No hostile fire on this front.	Totals.
BOUT DEVILLE	14/9.	—	Batteries fired between 30 & 40 rounds each registering various points in zones. Weather cloudy. No hostile fire on the Brigade.	Totals
BOUT DEVILLE	15/9.	—	Batteries continued registrational firing. Weather also in morning, fine in afternoon. No hostile fire on Brigade.	Totals
BOUT DEVILLE	16/9.	—	During the night 15/16 A & B Btys. sent their other section to gun positions. Instructional firing continued. Weather dull. No hostile fire. Front very quiet.	Totals

Army Form C. 2118.

WAR DIARY
INTELLIGENCE SUMMARY.

(Erase heading not required.)

Headquarters.
108th Bde. R.F.A.

Place	Date	Hour	Summary of Events and Information	Remarks and references to Appendices
	1915.			
BOUT DEVILLE	17.9.	—	Orders received (108/12) ordering us to proceed under cover of darkness to join IV Corps. Weather fine.	HHd. 108/12.
GRENAY.	18.9.	—	Marched from BOUT DEVILLE at 12.5 a.m. & reached NOEUX-LES-MINES at 5 a.m. (14½ miles) via BETHUNE. Wagon lines 1 mile W. of NOEUX-LES-MINES. Bde A.C. at LABUISSIÈRE.	HHd.
GRENAY.	19.9.	3.40 p	During the night A, C & D Batteries went into gun positions vacated by H & I Btys R.H.A. & Warwick R.H.A. B Bty is detached & put under the orders of Col. Poole, comdg 3rd Bde. R.G.A. The Brigade is in the "Counter Battery" Group which is also commanded by Col. Poole R.G.A. Battery positions in GRENAY. C Bty opened fire at 3 p.m. Came under fire of 4.2" Howitzers at 5½ p.m.	HHd.
GRENAY.	20.9.	—	B/108 moved into gun positions near Fosse 7. de Bethune (at h). A/108 ⅝" S of e in GRENAY. C/108 & D/108 1⅛" S of A & T in HALTE No.II of GRENAY.	HHd. Map No.11. Lens. 1:100,000.

[P.T.O.]

Army Form C. 2118

WAR DIARY
INTELLIGENCE SUMMARY.
(Erase heading not required.)

Headquarters.
108th Bde. R.F.A.

Instructions regarding War Diaries and Intelligence Summaries are contained in F.S. Regs., Part II. and the Staff Manual respectively. Title pages will be prepared in manuscript.

Place	Date	Hour	Summary of Events and Information	Remarks and references to Appendices
	1915			
GRENAY.	20/9.(continued)		Bde A.C. at LABUISSIÈRE. Wagon Lines & "D" in Bde A.C. at NOEUX-LES-MINES. Bde. Headquarters were shelled most of the day by 4.2" Howitzers & 7.7 mm. S.m.i. At 2.15 p.m. while engaging some wounded men Colonel H.T. Butcher, commanding the Brigade was killed. Major the Hon. R.G.A. Hamilton, Master of Belhaven & Stenton, R.F.A. then assumed command the Brigade. Weather fine.	Map N°.II. Lens. 1:100,000. H.B.J. H.B.J.
GRENAY.	21/9.	—	Orders for deliberate bombardment of GERMAN lines were received. Verbal orders from Col. POOLE cmdg Counter Batteries to open fire at dawn. Orders etc attacked & marked 108/3. Bombardment 21st, 22nd, 23rd & 24th to 4 days 100 rounds per gun, 25th & 26th 150 rounds per gun to be used. Batteries engaged targets near LOOS & ST PIERRE during the day. A machine gun was silenced by fire from C Btys at 10.15 p.m.	H.B.J. 108/3 H.B.J.

Army Form C. 2118. 7.

WAR DIARY
or
INTELLIGENCE SUMMARY.
(Erase heading not required.)

Headquarters.
108th Bde. R.F.A.

Place	Date	Hour	Summary of Events and Information	Remarks and references to Appendices
GRENAY.	1915. 22/9.	—	Batteries continued to shell hostile Batteries near LOOS and ST PIERRE. Being in the "Counter Battery" group we only fire on hostile batteries. "B/108" is allowed to fire 75 rounds per gun and the other batteries diminished in proportion. German artillery have been very quiet all day. The weather still holds fine.	HPS.
GRENAY.	23/9.	8 a.m.	Hostile artillery fire (8" Howitzer) was kept up near D/108 for one hour about 20 shells falling. On application to III Heavy Brigade R.G.A. this fire was quickly silenced. Our Batteries fired on LOOS area & ST PIERRE area most of the day. Hostile fire was very feeble. Weather turned cloudy towards 3 p.m. Thunder storm at 7 p.m. Wxxxxxxxxxxxxx High explosive shells have now been received & seem to be satisfactory.	HPS.

WAR DIARY
INTELLIGENCE SUMMARY.
(Erase heading not required.)

Army Form C. 2118

Headquarters.
108th Bde. R.F.A.

Place	Date	Hour	Summary of Events and Information	Remarks and references to Appendices
	1915			
GRENAY	24.9.	—	Brigade continued to engage LOOS & ST PIERRE area. Very heavy firing all afternoon. Feeble reply on O.Ps. by B.ys. of our guns. Very cloudy. This combined with smoke & dust raised by our fire made observation extremely difficult.	WD 108/4
GRENAY	25.9.	8.15am	At 5.50 fire was opened by our Batteries on targets indicated in attached list marked 108/4. Zero being at 5.50 a.m. Bombardment as directed was carried out. At 7.30 a.m. orders were received to fire on northern portion of ST PIERRE. This was done by C & D B.tys for 10 minutes. At 6 p.m. Orders (marked 108/5 attached) were received. At 9 p.m. the Brigade marched off picking up B B.ty on the road.	WD 108/4 108/5
LE ROUTOIR	26.9.	—	Positions were reconnoitred at 1 a.m. near LE ROUTOIR. At 2 a.m. Batteries came into action & dug in. Attached orders	WD 108/6 108/6

Army Form C.2118.9.

WAR DIARY or INTELLIGENCE SUMMARY

(Erase heading not required.)

Headquarters
108th Bde R.F.A.

Place	Date	Hour	Summary of Events and Information	Remarks and references to Appendices
	1915			
LE ROUTOIR	26.9.	(continued)	at 10 a.m. received Brigade orders on enemy's position, an attack was to be made at 11 a.m. F.O.O. line run out but from 11 a.m. no orders were received by the Brigade except that our form part of the left group & are under B'Gd Counter Temporarily. (marked 108/7)	H.Q.R.S. 108/7.
LE ROUTOIR	27.9.	—	Great difficulty in getting supplies & rations. Refilling point in Le Maisnil but at 2 p.m. verbal orders were received from "1st/8th to form a Barrage of fire from 3 to 3.5 at Hulluch in rear of G.O.C. 1 Guards Brigade. Fire was carried on at the rate of 2 rounds per battery per minute. Right ones laid out on roads S. of HULLUCH. Casualties, other ranks killed 1, wounded 3. About 15 horses have been killed. Weather dull.	H.Q.R.S. 108/8. 108/9.
LE ROUTOIR	28.9.	—	Batteries opened fire at 3.45 p.m. to support Infantry attack A, B & C Batteries were located out by 8th German Howitzers & were heavily shelled. 2/Lt C.A. Coldwells was killed and	H.Q.R.S.

WAR DIARY
INTELLIGENCE SUMMARY.
(Erase heading not required.)

Army Form C. 2118. No. 10.

Headquarters.
105th Bde. R.F.A.

Place	Date	Hour	Summary of Events and Information	Remarks and references to Appendices
	1915-			
LE ROUTOIR	28.9.		(continued) Capt. J.H. Edmond seriously wounded & 2.Lt. H.W. Jennings wounded. Besides these casualties 5 other ranks were killed & 16 wounded. The Brigade was forced temporarily into 3 gun Batteries. C Bty had one gun destroyed. Verbal orders received to move gun positions.	HRS.
NOYELLES.	29.9.	—	B & C Btys moved to new positions W of VERMELLES — LENS road, 2500× NW of LOOS. D remained at LE ROUTOIR.	HRS.
NOYELLES.	30.9.	—	D Bty joined B & C Btys & came into action by 10ᵗ. The Brigade now forms part of the Guards Division Left Group under Col. CARTWRIGHT. R.F.A.	HRS.

HRSentelle Capt. R.F.A.

Adjt. 105 Bde R.F.A.

APPENDICES

108/1 to 109/1.

"A" Form.
MESSAGES AND SIGNALS.
Army Form C. 2121.

TO: 106 & 108 F A Brigades

Sender's Number: BM 29 Day of Month: 9/9/15

Under instructions from 11th Corps
Reference ARRAS & HAZEBROUK Maps
106th and 108th Brigades (less
their SAA section of Brigade Ammunition
Columns) will march tomorrow 10th
and will be attached to Indian Corps
On 10th both brigades will march to LAIRES
On 11th both brigades will march to AIRE
(about 10 miles NE of LAIRES) via ESTRÉE BLANCHE
On 12th both brigades will march to
HAVERSKERQUE (about 8 miles east
of AIRE) via THIENNES
Billetting party will report in advance
On 11th to Town Mayor AIRE
On 12th to OC 19th Amn Sub Park HAVERSKERQUE
On arrival at HAVERSKERQUE both brigades
will come under orders of Indian Corps

"A" Form.
MESSAGES AND SIGNALS.
Army Form C. 2121.

they will be rationed up to
and for twelfth inst.
Route for tomorrows march - both brigades
via ROYON - CREQUY - FRUGES to LAIRES
106th to start 9 a.m.
108th to start 8.30 a.m. and to follow 106

Feeding strengths to be sent to this office
tomorrow morning.
Please acknowledge.

Colonel Butcher will command the force

From BM 24 DA
Place Hq
Time 8.30 pm

BM 24 DA

"A" Form. — Army Form C. 2121.
MESSAGES AND SIGNALS.

Prefix — Code 11·43 A·m — Words 43 — Charge —
This message is on a/c of:
Recd. at _____ m.
Date 108/2
From _____

CRA
Priority

TO — O.C 108 Bde RFA

Sender's Number: *BM163 — Day of Month: 17 — In reply to Number: — AAA

108 Bde RFA will march on night 17/18th under cover of darkness to 4th corps where it will come under orders of that core in releif of H16 and warwick batteries RHA AAA O.C. Bde to report to BGRA 4 corps as early as possible AAA batteries will be rationed up to and for 19th inst please ackowledge receipt

From: ~~Lahore~~ Lahore Divisonal
Place: Artillery
Time: 11·45 AM

SECRET

_____ Brigade R.H.A.

....xxx....

In accordance with 1st Army No. G.S. 164/3 (d) 10th September '15.

The number of rounds available for the forthcoming operations will be as follows :-

   13pr H.E. 354
   " Shrap. 544

   18pr H.E. 230
   " Shrap. 682

These numbers are allotted on the rough basis, for calculation -

   4 days deliberate bombardment
   2 days battle; and
   4 days subsequent fighting.

H.Q. IVth Corps Arty.   George Boscawen Captain R.F.A.
11th Septr. '15   Staff Officer IVth Corps Arty.

IVth C&A./22

SECRET

7th Brigade R.H.A.

AMMUNITION

1. In accordance with 1st Army instructions No.Q.343 the following number of rounds in excess of establishment may be drawn before the forthcoming operations begin :-

	Rounds per gun.
2.75 gun	100
13pr "	135
15pr "	80
18pr " H.E. -	30
18pr " S. -	70
4.5 How. H.E.	60
5" How.	60
6" How. H.E.	60
6" How. S.	35

Notification as to the date when this ammunition can be drawn will be issued later. This ammunition until required will be divided up between the echelons.

2. Batteries will dump ammunition at the gun positions as follows :-

13pr, 18pr, 15pr, 4.5 How. and 5" How. batteries - All ammunition carried in the gun limbers, firing battery wagons and 1st line wagons.

Total for each nature of gun.	
13pr and 18pr	176 rounds
15pr	250 rounds
4.5" How.	108 rounds
5" How.	176 rounds.
6" How.	100 rounds.

It is anticipated that this will admit of subsequent replenishment taking place only at night.

3. It is to be distinctly understood that no unexpended ammunition is to be replaced from the Parks.

Battery wagons and Bde.Amm.Cols will be replenished from the Div.Amm.Col., but the latter will remain partially empty.

4. At 6 p.m. daily, demands should be sent back to replace all expended ammunition, which should be sent up to the guns as soon as possible.

H.Q. IVth Corps Arty.

7th September 15.

George Boscawen, Captain R.A.
Staff Officer IVth Corps Arty.

SECRET

C.A.A/22

Reference IVth Corps Artillery C.A. 22 dated 7th September 1915.

In accordance with 1st Army instructions No.G.S.164/3 (d) of 10th September 1915 -

Insert :- in para 3 (C.A.22)

" No ammunition will be drawn until the rounds issued in excess of establishment (para.1. C.A.22) have been fired, after which ammunition will be drawn to replace expenditure, that is to say, to the extent necessary to keep all echelons in front of railhead up to establishment.

H.Q.IVth Corps Arty.
11th Septr.15

George Boscawen   Captain R.F.A.
Staff Officer IVth Corps Arty.

SECRET.

~~"MAGHASHTAN" Group.~~
~~"MASSY" Group.~~
7th Brigade R.H.A.
~~47th London D.A.C.~~
5th London F.A.B.

Reference my S.C.C. 522.

These instructions re ammunition are not being carried out in accordance with para 3.

Several cases have arisen of batteries dumping ammunition at the guns and of the B.A.C's and D.A.C. filling up, with the result that the establishment of rounds per gun carried in the Batteries, B.A.C. and D.A.C. has been exceeded by the number of rounds dumped.

Serious complaints have been received from 4th Corps regarding this, and the G.O.C.R.A. directs that more care is to be taken in reading orders, and to see that they are strictly carried out, and that any surplus is to be adjusted and returned to the Park at once.

The number of rounds stated in my S.C.C. 522, para 2, is to be dumped at the guns forthwith.

This will mean :-

(1) In the case of 13 Prs. Battery wagons and gun limbers will be filled up from the B.A.C. and that the establishment of the B.A.C. will be reduced, as long as the dumping exists, by the number of rounds dumped at the guns.

(2) In the case of 18 Prs. Battery wagons and gun limbers will be filled up from the B.A.C. and D.A.C., which will leave the D.A.C. empty and the B.A.C. partially filled only, the number of rounds ~~being advanced~~ *short* in these two echelons being the number of rounds in the dump. This state of affairs will last so long as the dump exists.

(3) In the case of 4.5" and 5" Howitzers. Battery wagons and gun limbers will be filled up as far as possible, and the B.A.C. and D.A.C. will be empty so long as the dump exists.

(4) In the case of the 18 Prs. Battery wagons and gun limbers and also 5th London B.A.C. will be filled up. The reduction of rounds carried in the echelon's wagons due to the number of rounds dumped at the guns being borne entirely by the D.A.C. (2592 rounds) and the 6th London B.A.C. (408 rounds) whose establishment will therefore be reduced to 456 rounds. This state of affairs will last so long as the dump exists.

These instructions are to be carried out at once, and on no account is ammunition to be requisitioned by one echelon from another until the ammunition has been expended, and then the requisitions are only to be for number of rounds expended. Ammunition to replace the expended ammunition will be drawn in the usual way and forwarded through the echelons in accordance with my S.C.C. 459.

Orders have already been issued to the effect that the 13th and 14th London Batteries draw their ammunition (No. 80 fuze) from the 5th London F.A.B., and that the 12th London Battery will draw their ammunition (No. 85 fuze, as long as available, after which No. 65 fuzes) from the 6th London B.A.C.

Harold Hale
Major,
Staff Captain.
47th Divl. Arty.

S.C.C. 781.
13/9/15.

10819.

Headquarters,

   7th Bde. R.H.A.

      I am sending you herewith copy of the arrangements for gun ammunition supply for our batteries, together with traffic map, which may be useful to you.

Harold Hale.
          Major,
          Staff Captain.
          47th Divl. Arty.

S.C. 695
12/9/15.

    O.C. H Bty RHA   E/S.
        J   " "   JM
        War " "   LAS.G.
    7th Bde A.C.   RMB

Please pass quickly.
The route for 7th Bde RHA will be the same as that shewn for G Battery RHA.

                     W.R. Banister
                      Capt
                 Adjt 7th Bde RHA

O.C. D Bty.   seen H.B.W. for Capt. Bush
      E "
      A "   seen JB
      C "   seen HH
Bde A.C.

SECRET.

To Headquarters,
~~47th (Lon) Division.~~
....

ARRANGEMENTS FOR GUN AMMUNITION SUPPLY.

(Reference TRAFFIC MAP, dated 11/9/15)
(Copy attached)

DISPOSITION OF B.A.C.'s and WAGON LINES.

1. (a) The present position of the B.A.C.'s and Wagon Lines are as follows:-

    B.A.C.'s

"G" Battery, R.H.A.	HAILLICOURT.
25th.Brigade, R.F.A.	"
39th.Brigade, R.F.A.	"
5th.Lon.Bde.R.F.A.	"
8th.Lon.Bde.R.F.A.	"
25th.Brigade, R.G.A.	AUCHEL.

    WAGON LINES.

"G" Battery, R.H.A.	K.23.b. and c.
25th.Brigade, R.F.A.	DROUVIN WOODS.
39th.Brigade, R.F.A.	"
5th.Lon.Bde.R.F.A.	"
8th.Lon.Bde.R.F.A.	"

    (b) An advanced Echelon for the Wagon Lines (except "G" Battery) consisting of 6 wagons per 6 gun battery and 4 wagons per 4 gun battery, will be established at Point "D" in the CORONS, S.E. of NOEUX-LES-MINES. The wagons will stand, and the horses will be picketed in the streets well under cover behind the houses. Horses can be watered in these streets from existing stand-pipes connected to the Town Supply.
    Owing to the 15 Pr. and 5" How. B.A.C.'s being equipped with G.S. wagons, the remaining wagons of 3 15 Pr. batteries (namely 12th., 13th. and 14th. Lon.Batteries) and 2 5" How. batteries (namely 21st. and 22nd.Lon.(How) Batteries) at DROUVIN will move to HAILLICOURT and be attached to their respective B.A.C.'s and will be used for taking ammunition from B.A.C. G.S. wagons to Advanced Wagon lines.

    (c) Six 3-ton motor lorries of the 25th.Brigade, R.G.A. (40 rounds per gun) will form an Advanced Echelon and will stand about Point "E" in one of the streets in the CORONS referred to in No.1 (b).

SYSTEM ADOPTED FOR SUPPLY.

2. (a) <u>D.A.C. to B.A.C.'s.</u>

    The ammunition Refilling Point is at Point "A" from which B.A.C.'s at Point "B" will fill up. Ammunition wagons will proceed to B.A.C.'s at Point "B" by road (not shown on Traffic Map) through LABUISSIERE and thence by main East Road No.1, returning by Road No.22 and 21.

(b) "G" Battery, R.H.A.

   (i) B.A.C. to Wagon Line.

   Ammunition wagons will proceed from HAILLICOURT by Roads No.1 and No.4. Ammunition will be carried across Road No.18 to battery wagons and empty ammunition wagons will then return along Roads No.18 and No.20 across stubble fields behind HAILLICOURT Mine.

   (ii) Wagon Line to Battery.

   Ammunition wagons will proceed via Roads No.3, 5, 6, 7, 10 and 23 and will return via Roads No.23, 10, 12, 14, 15, and 18.

(c) 18 Prs., 15 Prs., and 5" Howitzers.

   (i) B.A.C.'s to Advanced Wagon Line.

   Ammunition wagons will proceed from HAILLICOURT via Roads No.1, &2, to the west side of the CORONS. Full wagons will be exchanged for empty wagons which will return by Roads 16, 18, and 19 or 20. Limbered wagons only should be used as these will save changing ammunition from one wagon to another at Point "D".

   (ii) Advanced Wagon Line to Batteries.

   Ammunition wagons will proceed via Roads No.16, 17, and 6 to MAZINGARBE. From this point batteries on the Northern part of the section will proceed via Roads No.18, 24, and 9, and batteries on the Southern part of the section via Roads No.7, 10 and 23.
   All wagons returning will proceed via Roads No.10, 12, 14, 15, and 2 to Point "D".

(d) Wagons at Point "F".

   It is not proposed to use the wagons at the Wagon Lines at Point "F" for the normal supply of ammunition. These wagons, together with the gun limbers, will be kept full.

(e) 25th. Siege Brigade, R.G.A.

   Ammunition lorries will proceed from Ammunition Column to Advanced Echelon at Point "E" via Roads No. 1, 3, 17, 16, returning by Roads No.16, 17 and 21.
   Ammunition lorries from Point "E" will proceed via Roads No.16, 17, 6, and 7 for 23rd. Siege Battery, R.G.A. by Roads No.10, returning by Roads No.11, 16, 17 and 21.
   The Advanced Echelon at Point "E" should always have its full complement of 6 wagons.

COMMUNICATIONS. 3. The following arrangements have been made with Divisional Signals for quick communications:-

   (a) Batteries to Points "C", "D", and "E".
   (b) Points "C", "D" and "E" to Point "B".
   (c) Batteries to Point "F".

   (a) Batteries can telegraph to Group H.Q. Group H.Q. can send telegraph messages from LES BREBIS Signals to NOEUX-LES-MINES Signals via 47th. Div. H.Q.

Cyclist Orderlies from Points "C","D", and "E" should be kept at NOEUX-LES-MINES Signal Office to carry messages to their respective units.

(b) Messages can be sent to NOEUX-LES-MINES Signal Office, and will be transmitted by Signals to their Signal Station which will be established in central position (which will be notified later) for all B.A.C.'s. B.A.C.'s should have Cyclist Orderlies at this Central Signal Station.

(c) Messages from Batteries can be transmitted through Group H.Q. and LES BREBIS Signals direct to Central Point (which will be notified later) to the Wagon Lines at Point "F".

By these arrangements ammunition can be got up to Batteries at short notice, and gun limbers can also be sent for quickly. Divisional Signals have promised to send all these messages "PRIORITY" immediately they are handed in.

Harold Hale
Major,
Staff Captain, for
Brigadier-General,
Comdg. 47th.(Lon) Divl.Artillery.

S.C. c/459.
11/9/15.

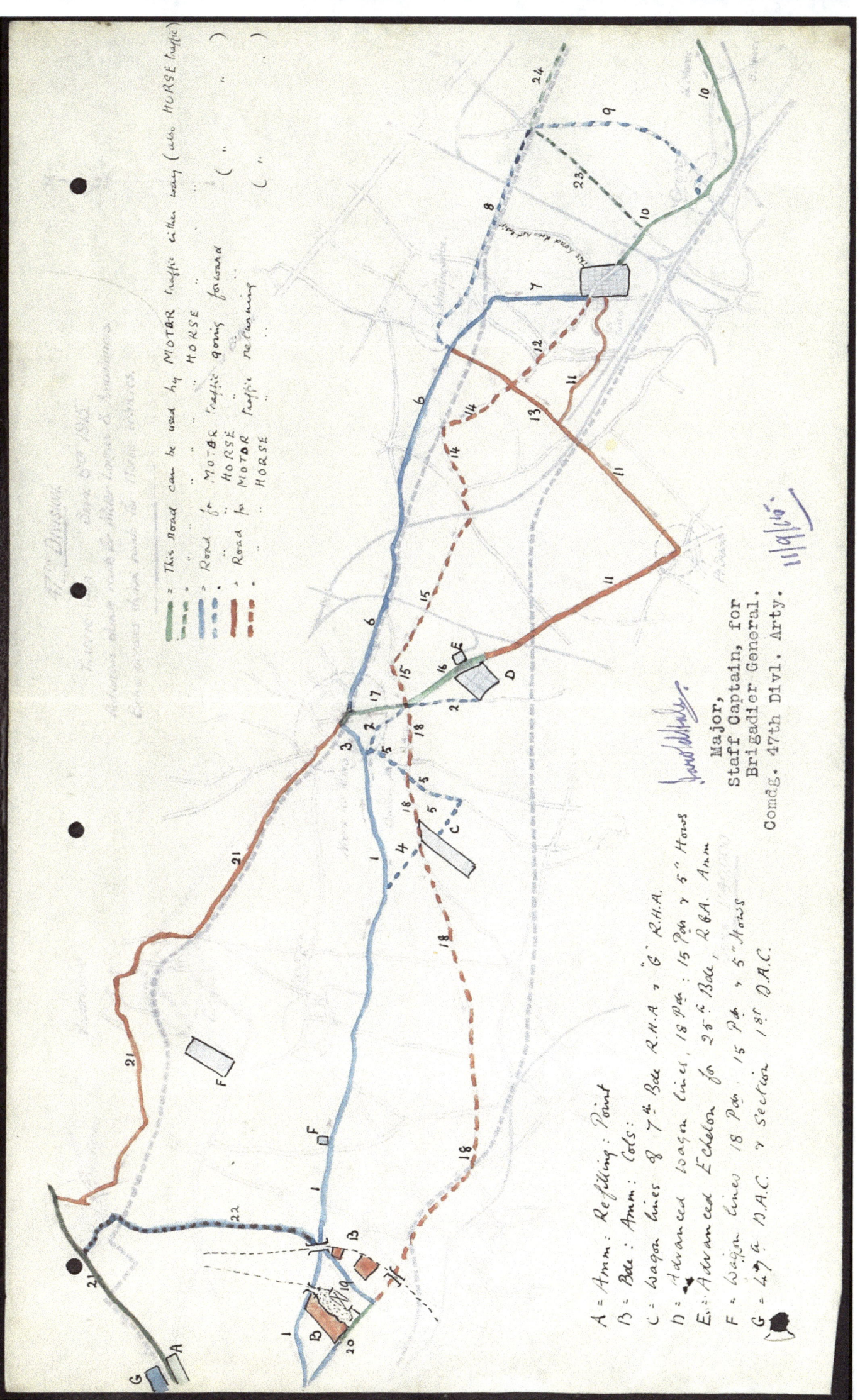

SECRET   E.H. 31

108/4

108 Bde R.F.A.

at time to be notified later which
will be 0hrs. 00 min. Fire will be opened
as under.

0.00 } A 108   G 35 b+d + G 36
to 0.40 } C 108   Puits 11 & ST. PIERRE
          D 108   Wood in M 6 a + gun positions

A steady rate of neutralizing fire to
be kept up - ammn. allowed 100 rds per battery.

0.40 } A 108   ready for batteries E of LOOS
to 0.50 } C 108   "   "   "   in ST. PIERRE
          D 108   "   "   "   ST. PIERRE + Puits 12

Ammn. as required

1.00   Cease firing

0.00 } B 108   A steady rate of fire on
to 0.40 }   HULLUCH Valley
          Ammn. allowed 200 rds.
After 0.40 cease fire.

E. Pulley Blackwood
Capt. R.F.A.
Adj. 3rd Bde R.F.A.

24/9/15.
(June 5.50 am. H.S.)

"A" Form.   Army Form C. 2121.
MESSAGES AND SIGNALS.   No. of Message_____

Prefix____Code____m.	Words	Charge	This message is on a/c of:	Recd. at____m.
Office of Origin and Service Instructions.	Sent			Date 10 8/5
	At____m.		____Service.	From____
	To____			
	By____		(Signature of "Franking Officer.")	By____

TO { 108 7A Bde

Sender's Number	Day of Month	In reply to Number	
BM 75	26/9/15		AAA

Artillery of 21st & 24th Divisions will be in position in observation by 5.30 a.m. this morning with object of bombarding German trench extending from H 26 b 8.8 to H 14 c 8 2

24th Div Art will be south of VERMELLES — HULLOCH Road and north of ~~line~~ track running from G 17 d.1.2. — G 18 c cross roads G 19 a 7.7. 21st Div Art. will be south of latter line.

Objective 108th German trench from H 26 b 8.8 ~~to~~ H 20 d 4.3. exclusive of redoubt 107th ~~H 20 d 4.3 One battery~~ half from H 20 d 4.3 to H 20 d. 4.6.

From
Place
Time

The above may be forwarded as now corrected. (Z)
Censor.   Signature of Addressor or person authorised to telegraph in his name.
* This line should be erased if not required.

"A" Form. Army Form C. 2121.
MESSAGES AND SIGNALS.
No. of Message_____

Prefix ____ Code ____ m.	Words	Charge	*This message is on a/c of :	Recd. at ____ m.
Office of Origin and Service Instructions.				Date ____
	Sent		____ Service	From ____
	At ____ m.			
	To			
	By	(Signature of "Franking Officer.")	By ____

TO { _____ Centre _____ }

* Sender's Number | Day of Month | In reply to Number | **AAA**

Objectives

109 Brigade all batteries will concentrate on redoubt in H20d

108 Brigade from H26 b 8.8 to H20 d 5.2

107th One battery from H20 d 3.5 to H 20 b/d
Remainder of 107 from H20 d 5.2 to H20 d 5.5

B.A.C. will not advance E. of front line of trenches recently held by British till further orders.

From	
Place	
Time	

The above may be forwarded as now corrected. (Z)

Censor. Signature of Addressor or person authorised to telegraph in his name.

* This line should be erased if not required.

"A" Form.
MESSAGES AND SIGNALS.
Army Form C. 2121.

TO: Corps

Brigade R.F.C. Commander
will meet B.M. 24 Div Arty
at 5 a.m. at cross roads
just W of La ROUTOIRE
Copies to 107 108 &
109 Bdes R.F.A.
Bdes are now under orders of G.O.C.
R.A.

From: B M 24 DA
Place:
Time: 3.15 p.m.

"A" Form. Army Form C. 2121.
MESSAGES AND SIGNALS. No. of Message_____

Prefix___ Code___m.	Words	Charge	This message is on a/c of:	Recd. at___m.
Office of Origin and Service Instructions.				Date 10/8/6
	Sent			From
	At___m.		___Service.	
	To___			
	By___		(Signature of "Franking Officer.")	By

TO { 108 FA Bde

Sender's Number: BM 78a 26   Day of Month   In reply to Number   **AAA**

Our infantry are holding the general line of the enemy's old front line trenches, with a sharp salient towards the enemy as far as G 18 b central. These trenches are to be held. The Guards Division are in reserve on our right.

* Hulluch
  G 18 b   The sketch represents our line

Our cavalry are in LOOS
Capt Nolthorpe 72 Inf Bde Staff Captain should on now leave be called and brought an officer 108 to remain at Bde HQ.
72 Bde H.Q. are 300x E of LONE TREE

From BM   24 DA
Place
Time 7.55 A.M.

The above may be forwarded as now corrected. (Z)   JP Hanway Major
Censor. Signature of Addressee or person authorised to telegraph in his name.
* This line should be erased if not required.   BM 24 DA

108/7.

26/9/15 — 11.50 AM

Have given your note to
S.O. 24th Divn

You are temporarily under
Lt Col Coates who will give
any necessary orders if
you have not already got
in touch with Left Bde
Commander & receive orders
from him.

J Shea
BGGS

108/8

Code
BK/M   CDR   48
OC 108 RFA
    BDE
────────────────────
GFX2   27th   AAA

Please report yourself
personally to BGC FIRST
GUARDS BRIGADE FIELDING
whose HQ are at about
G 23 here 65 in the
trenches as soon as
possible AAA Guards
HQ signals are obtaining
wire for your F.O.O.'s
AAA Please acknowledge

adjt 107-FA BDE
    2.37 PM   3

Guards Division

Left Group Operation Order No I
By Lt Col I R Coates, Commanding Left Group.
Ref. Trench Map 1/10,000

1. Intention. Guards Div. will attack as follows
   2nd Guards Brigade. First objective CHALK PIT H25 a
                       Second -.- KEEP & PUITS 14 bis
   3rd Guards Brigade objective   HILL 70 & redoubt.
   after 2nd objective of 2nd GUARDS BDE. This is to be
   called the 3rd objective. This attack will be delivered through
   LOOS

2. Times for attack.
   1st Objective - 4 pm.
   2nd Objective - 4.20 pm
   3rd Objective - 4.50 pm
   The 1st Guards Brigade will cooperate with fire on
   their left.

2. Tasks for Left Group is as per attached
   programmes.
   Time tables must be strictly adhered to.

3. Rate of fire will generally be slow. Unless
   tactical situation demands a faster rate, fire
   shd be irregular not exceeding two rounds
   per gun per minute.

4. OC 100/F.A/Bde will be in personal touch with
   BGC 1st Guards Brigade.

5. Report Centre Guards Division HQ.

                              [signature]
                              Lt RFA
                              for Col I R Coates

	Unit	Tasks	Notes
3 – 5 pm	Left Group 108 FA/18R 18pr	H.13 c 4.2. to H.19 c 8.6, 200ⁿ S of Jn 80	All pre-arranged Star shells
3 – 4 pm	1 Bde (5 batteries) 106 FA/18R 18pr	H.19 c 8.6. to keep 14 hr (eval) & shelling CHALK PIT HOUSE	Total 6 Batteries required R – 2 A = 4 /109 in reserve
3 – 4.20 pm	1 Bar 18 pr	KEEP (eval) – Continue 55 – 418 to shelling H.21 d 2.1. to H.31 6.2.7. (at Col. ruler battery)	A 109
3 – 4 pm	1 How Bty A 109	Mower H.19 a.6.6.	C 109
3 – 4 pm	So – C 109 Right Group 1 Bde	CHALK PIT House.	
	1 Bde	Hill 70 Garrison & responsible that all wire in cut & will support 3 Gds. Bde. attack if 76 Bde is not up. O.C. will report to 3 Gds Bde.	
		Support 2 Guards Bde Left F G.O.C 2ⁿ Guards Bde at Le RUTOIRE	
	2 How Bty	R/Gp. H.31 6.2.s. – 29¹ L at Bn, H.31b.2.9.2. – A side d.t. 7. ½ mins report F GOC 2 Gds Bn LE RUTOIRE	
	1 Siege Bty	½ how OC 135 Siege F OCRA LE RUTOIRE	

"A" Form. Army Form C. 2121.
MESSAGES AND SIGNALS. No. of Message

Prefix	Code	m.	Words	Charge	This message is on a/c of:	Reed. at ... m.
	of Origin and Service Instructions.					Date
			Sent		Service.	From 108/9
			At ... m.			
			To			
			By		(Signature of "Franking Officer.")	By

TO OC 108/FA/BDe

| Sender's Number. | Day of Month. | In reply to Number | AAA |
| GF x 8 | 27. | | |

You will lay out night lines on the front opp to your adjt. Keep touch with battalions to front. Open fire only in case of heavy shelling to your own front — Sh'd this happen you will fire no no immediately

From SO Left Group
Place
Time 8.57 pm

(Z)

BRIGADE ORDERS.

Orders by Col. H.T. Butcher. R.F.A.　　　　No. 2.
5/9/15.

7. Orderlies	An Orderly will be on duty at Brigade Headquarters at all times (night and day) from each Battery and the A.C. In addition to this the Battery on duty will supply a bicycle Orderly from 7 a.m. until 8 p.m. These Orderlies will bring their day's rations with them.
8. Alarm Post.	In the event of an alarm the Brigade will form up on Column of route on the road MARLES-NEUVILLE. Head of the Column will be at the house LA CHARTREUSE, ½" S. of E in NEUVILLE. Brigade will form up in the order A, B, C, D Btys, followed by the Amm. Col.
9. Police.	The Battery on duty will find one N.C.O. and 3 men as Intelligence Police. Their duties are to prevent espionage. The N.C.O. will report to the 71st. Inf. Bde. Hdqrs. for detailed instructions.
10. Smoking.	Men must not be allowed to smoke in barns on account of danger of fire.
11. Cashier.	The Field Cashier will be at the 71st. Inf. Bde. Hdqrs. at 2.30 on Wednesday next.
12. Casualties.	Casualties to either horses or men which entail evacuating will be reported to this Office at once.
13. Equipment.	Buffers are to be bound with the ropes provided for the purpose without delay. The lettering on all vehicles is to be made clearly legible at once.
14. Discipline.	Some men have been seen wearing caps comforters on duty. This must cease at once.
15. Billetting.	O.C's Batteries and Amm. Col. will render a return by 6 p.m. on Sundays showing the number of Officers accomodated at 1 franc per night, (2) Other ranks. Total number accomodated with beds at 20 centimes per night. (3) Other ranks, Total number accomodated with shelter only at 5 centimes per night. In the event of a move being ordered O.C's will render a report at once to the Adjutant showing the number of Officers and men who have been billetted in the place either from arrival or from last return if applying to same billetting area.

H.E. Whittle,
Capt. R.F.A &
Adjutant 108th. Brigade R.F.A.

Orders by Col. H.T.Butcher.R.F.A.   No.3.
6/9/15.

16. Returns.

Batteries and A.C. will render a return by 8 p.m. daily showing any casualties that have occurred during the day or previous night. Nil returns will be rendered.

XXXXXXXXXXX

A.F. B231 will only be required on Fridays by 6 p.m. and not as formerly ordered.

17. Cashier.

The Field Cashier will be at the following places on Tuesday the 7th. inst.
    H.Q. Supply Column. BEAURAINVILLE.   2 p.m.
    H.Q. 8th. Bedford Regiment. NEUVILLE.   4 p.m.
    Representatives of units requiring advances will attend at the most convenient place. The Field Cashier will not visit the 71st. Brigade on Wednesday as previously arranged.

18. Divisional Exercise.

There will be a Divisional Exercise to-morrow.

H S Wintele
Capt.R.F.A.
Adjutant 108th. Brigade R.F.A.

19. Trees.

Horses and Mules are not to be tied to trees or fences and they must be picketted at such a distance that they cannot gnaw the bark. (To be copied in all Battery Orders.)

Orders by Col. H.T.Butcher.R.F.A.　　　　No.4.

7/9/15.

20. Bathing.	O.C's units will take steps to prevent any bathing in dangerous parts of the River CANCHE, owing to the weeds.
21. Blankets.	Unit Commanders will indent for 1 blanket per man at once.
22. Orderlies.	The Orderlies furnished to R.A. Headquarters, by Units will remain both day and night. Should any Orderly be sent out late to his own Unit, the C.O. may replace him by another man, but he should bring with him a note to this effect.
23. War Diaries.	War Diaries will be commenced at once if not already started
24. Iron Rations.	Batteries and A.C. will render a report to this Office by 10 a.m. to-morrow stating whether they are in possession of full Iron Rations or not.
25. Attached men of A.V.C.	Batteries and A.C. will render a return by noon to-morrow giving the following details of the A.V.C. men who are attached to them. Corps No. in full. Date of enlistment. Rank and name.(surname first.) Rate of allotment known to O.C. Name and address of allottee, if known to O.C.

Capt.R.F.A.
Adjutant 108th. Brigade R.F.A.

26. Promotion.　　No.　　Br. Hughes to be Corporal with effect from 7th. August 1915.

Orders by Col. H.T.Butcher.R.F.A.　　　No.5.

8/9/15.

27. Lecture.	All Battery Quartermaster Sergeants will be at the 71st. Infantry Brigade Headquarters to-morrow at 11.30 a.m.
28. Orderly.	In future the Orderly for 24th. Divisional Artillery Headquarters will be found by the Battery next for duty. This will be a bicycle Orderly and not a mounted Orderly and not a mounted orderly as previously ordered.
29. Divine Service.	There will be Divine Service on Sunday next at the same place as last Sunday at 10 a.m. Batteries and A.C. will march to the Service independently. There will be a voluntary parade for Holy Communion at 12 noon on Sunday. Place will be notified later.

Capt.R.F.A.
Adjutant 108th. Brigade R.F.A.

Orders by Col. H.T. Butcher. R.F.A.   No.6.

9/9/15.

30. Surplus Forage. — In the Event of a move, Batteries will leave any surplus forage which will be collected by the A.S.C. Not more than one sack of oats is allowed to be carried on any wagon. Attention is called to the circular letter re overloading vehicles.

31. Bounds. — N.C.O's and men will not leave the village after 7 p.m.

32. Officers. — Officers will make arrangements so that if they are away at any time they will be able to be sent for in case of urgent orders.

H.S. Suttele,
Capt. R.F.A.
Adjutant 108th. Brigade R.F.A.

Orders by Col. H.T.Butcher.R.F.A.   No.7.

10/9/15.

33. March.
The Brigade will march to XXX AIRE to-morrow. Order of march. Hq., B Bty, C Bty, D Bty, A Bty, Bde. A.C. The head of the column will be at the cross roads ¼" W. of "B" in BANCOURT. XXXXXX Brigade will be ready to march off at 1.30 p.m.

34. Billetting Parties.
It is suggested that one Officer per Battery should accompany the Billetting Parties.

35. Orders.
Attention is called to Orders not being passed down from Battery to Battery when the Brigade when on the march. This leads to great inconvenience. In future Battery Commanders will be responsible that their Nos.1 pass all orders on and the last No.1 will see that the following Battery receives the order. All Brigade Orders will be preceded by the caution "Brigade Order" which MUST be repeated by all passing the order.

36. Pace of Marching.
If the pace of marching is found to be too fast for the rear Batteries, a report will be passed to the front to that effect.

Capt.R.F.A.
Adjutant 108th. Brigade R.F.A.

Orders by Col. H.T.Butcher.R.F.A.　　　No.8.
11/9/15.

37. March.
The Brigade will march to **HAVERSKIRQUE** via **THIENNES** to-morrow as follows:-
10.15 a.m. Headquarters and C Battery.
10.30 a.m. D Battery.
10.45 a.m. A Battery.
11 a.m. B Battery.
11.15 a.m. Bde. Amm. Col.

38. Promotion.
No.47939 @Br.Secker.W. Bde.A.C. is promoted to the rank of Corporal.

39. Board.
The following Officers will assemble to-morrow to inquire into the loss of a telephone. Time and place to be appointed by the president.
　　　President.　Capt.P.Y.Birch.R.A
　　　Members.　　2Lt.H.L.Webber.R.F.A.
　　　　　　　　　2Lt.L.B.Govan.R.F.A.

40. Billetting Parties.
Billetting Parties will parade with C Battery to-morrow.

Capt.R.F.A.
Adjutant 108th. Brigade R.F.A.

Orders by Col. H.T. Butcher. R.F.A. No. 9.
12/9/15.

IX

41. March.

The Brigade will march as follows to-morrow.

Hq., A Bty. and B Bty. at 10 a.m. to cross-roads ¼"
S. of S in la GORGUE STATION via the road MERVILLE-LA GORGUE.

C Bty, D Bty, and Bde. A.C. (under Capt. Miller) at 10.30 a.m. to cross-roads ¾" S.W. of L in LESTREM via the road through MERVILLE.

When moving to gun positions Batteries will not leave Wagon lines before 8 p.m.

Officers commanding C and D Batteries will meet Col. Maxwell at Hdqrs. 11th. Bde R.F.A. at BOUT-DEVILLE at 10 a.m.

Officers Commanding A and B Batteries will report to Officers Commanding 14th. Bty.R.F.A. and 44th. Bty. R.F.A. respectively during the afternoon.

Billetting parties of A and B Btys. will report to the Adjutant at 10 a.m. at the head of the column. An Officer from C, and D Btys. and the Bde. A.C. will report to the Staff Captain, Lahore Division at FOSSE at 10.30 a.m. These Officers will take billetting parties with them.

Officers commanding Batteries and A.C. will make arrangements for a N.C.O. to march with their Baggage wagons to guide them to their right places.

42. Returns.

The following returns will be rendered daily to the Adjutant. Place to be notified later.

(a) Casualty Return.
(b) Expenditure of Ammunition.
(c) Targets fired at and number of shells fired by hostile Batteries, position of hostile Batteries (if known) also size of shells.

These returns will be made up from 12 noon to 12 noon and rendered before 5 p.m. Battery Commanders will arrange to have these returns rendered punctually as they have to be forwarded to the Divisional Artillery Headquarters.

Capt R.F.A.
Adjutant 108th. Brigade R.F.A.

108th. Brigade Orders.   No.1.
----------------------   4/9/15.

1. **Estaminets.** These will be open from 11 a.m. to 1 p.m. and from 6 p.m. to 8 p.m.

2. **Billets.** All troops will be in billets by 9 p.m.

3. **Divine Service.** Batteries will make their own arrangements for holding Divine Service at 11.30 a.m. to-morrow.

5. **Police.** Batteries will make their own arrangements for Police duties. The Battery on duty for the week will furnish a N.C.O. to act as Provost Sergeant. He will report to the R.S.M. at the Brigade Office at 9 a.m. on Mondays for orders.

6. **Duty.** B Battery will be on duty for the week commencing 6/9/15.

                                               Capt. R.F.A.
                              Adjutant 108th. Brigade R.F.A.

Orders by Col. H.T.Butcher.R.F.A.   No.10.
13/9/15.

43. Straw. Not more straw than is allowed is to be taken from the inhabitants. If more is required it must be bought by the men privately. Allowance to be requisitioned for;- 8lbs. per man per week.

44. Returns. The returns mentioned in yesterday's orders will be ready for collection at 12.30 p.m. daily. Each Battery Orderly with Headquarters will be sent to his own Battery to collect these returns.

Capt.R.F.A.
Adjutant 108th. Brigade R.F.A.

Orders by Col. H.T.Butcher. R.F.A.　　　No. 11.
16/9/15.

45. Cashier.	Batteries and A.C. will draw any money they want for paying the troops etc. from the Cashier. British Troops. LOCON. (near LA FOSSE.)
46. Washing.	Clean changes of washing can be obtained from the Indian Corps Laundry on the LESTREM-LA GORGUE Road. An indent must be sent in stating the number of changes required. Dirty clothes must be returned on the following day.
47. Telephone Cables.	It is suggested that distinguishing marks should be got for the telephone cables. In the event of Batteries getting these the following colours will be used. Headquarters----------Red. A Bty.----------------Blue. B Bty.----------------White. C Bty.----------------Yellow. D Bty.----------------Blue and white. Labels are able to be bought with the designation of the unit on, colours as above.

[signature] Capt. R.F.A.
Adjutant 108th. Brigade R.F.A.

Orders by Col. H.T.Butcher. R.F.A.   No.12.
17/9/15.

48. March.
The Brigade will march to wagon lines near NOEUX-LES-MINES. (about 3 miles S. of BETHUNE&)
The Brigade will form up in the following order at 12 Midnight. Hq., D Bty., A Bty., B Bty., C Bty., and A.C. Head of the Brigade to be at cross-roads ¼" West of F in FOSSE. (ref. map. 1/40,000 HAZEBROUCK.)
One Officer per Battery with Billetting party will report to the Adjutant at the head of the Brigade before moving off.

49. Indents.
Batteries will indent for any articles broken or damaged at once.

Capt. R.F.A.
Adjutant 108th. Brigade R.F.A.

108th. Brigade Orders by
Major the Hon. R. Hamilton. R.F.A.

No. 18.

50. Drag Ropes.   All units having horse drawn vehicles, motor cars and ambulances on charge will submit indents to the D.A.D.O.S. for two light drag ropes per vehicle.

51. Photography.   As cases still occur of photographs being taken, attention is again directed to G.R.O. No. 464.
"Commanding Officers will take steps to see that any camera that may now be in the possession of any Officer or soldier, is returned immediately to England. Films or plates will be destroyed. Any Officer or soldier (or other person subject to Military Law) found in possession of a camera after Sept. 30th. 1915 will be placed in arrest and the case reported to G.H.Q. for instructions as to disposal.

52. Purchase of String.   Officers Commanding units may purchase locally at the rate of one yard per waterproof sheet on charge strong string. Submit the receipted bill to D.A.D.O.S. 24th. Division for the approval of G.O.C. the cost being included in the imprest account of the unit.

H.S.Winstone
Capt. R.F.A.
Adjutant 108th. Brigade R.F.A.

22/9/15.

The O.C.

    A, B, C, & D Btys. ~~Bde. A.C.~~ 108th. Bde. R.F.A.

    The matter of telephonists leaving their instruments or sleeping when on duty has become serious. In one case after getting no response from H.Q. the Battery telephonist stated that he had been away to get his breakfast.

    The following order is to be read out to every telephonist in the Brigade by an Officer who will certify in writing that he has done so and state the names of telephonists to whom it has been read. The above report is to reach this Office by 7 p.m. this evening 23/9/15 without fail.

> "All telephonists are warned that when on duty at their instruments they are in the same position as a sentry in the presence of the enemy. The penalty for a sentry sleeping on, or quitting his post when on active service is death. The extreme penalty has on several occasions been carried out during this war."

HEADQUARTERS
23 SEP 1915
108th. BRIGADE, R.F.A.
23/9/15.

                                        R. Hamilton

                                                Major. R.F.A.
                             Commanding 108th. Brigade R.F.A.

108th. Brigade Orders
by
Major the Hon. R. Hamilton. R.F.A.   No. 19.

53. Command.   Major the Honourable R.G.A. Hamilton, R.F.A. took over the command of the 108th. Brigade R.F.A. vice Col. H.T. Butcher, R.F.A.; killed in action 20/9/15.

54. Letters.   Official envelopes are not to be used for private letters. In future letters in these envelopes will be destroyed. Officers commanding units will see that this order is carried out.

55. Gas helmets.   Battery Commanders will see that every man in his unit is in possession of a smoke helmet. The man should keep it is his possession at all times.

[signature]
Capt. R.F.A.
Adjutant 108th. Brigade R.F.A.

13/9/15.

121/7008

24th Hussars.

108th Bde: R.F.A.
Vol: 2

Oct 15.

Army Form C. 2118.

WAR DIARY
or
INTELLIGENCE SUMMARY.

Vol. II

Headquarters 108th Bde. R.F.A.

(Erase heading not required.)

Instructions regarding War Diaries and Intelligence Summaries are contained in F. S. Regs., Part II. and the Staff Manual respectively. Title pages will be prepared in manuscript.

Map 1:10000 36c NW 3 & part of 1. Summary of Events and Information

Place	Date	Hour	Summary of Events and Information	Remarks and references to Appendices
	1915			
NOYELLES	1.10	7a—	The S.A.A. section of the B.A.C. received orders to join the 72nd Inf. Bde. near LILLERS at once. We now form part of the Left Group under Col. Cartwright R.F.A. and are attached to the Guards Divisional Artillery.	Appx.
NOYELLES	2.10	—	During the night we formed a Barrage of fire, orders attached 108/1 & 2. 108/1 & 2. Batteries were not fired on during the day although positions are in the open. Heavy hostile shelling on other batteries 200x in front of us.	108/1 & 2
NOYELLES	3.10	—	Barrage of fire continued during last night. Several salvoes were ordered to be fired into HULLUCH between 10 p. & 12 midnight. One section of D/105 was relieved by a section from the 72nd Bde R.F.A. at 9a.m. attached order 108/3. B.C. & D. completed orders were received re cutting wire. 108/4. Received to rejoin 24th Division. 108/4.	108/3. 108/4. Appx.

Army Form C. 2 2

WAR DIARY
or
INTELLIGENCE SUMMARY.
(Erase heading not required.)

Headquarters.
105 Bde, R.F.A.

Instructions regarding War Diaries and Intelligence Summaries are contained in F. S. Regs., Part II. and the Staff Manual respectively. Title pages will be prepared in manuscript.

Place	Date	Hour	Summary of Events and Information	Remarks and references to Appendices
	1915.			
VIEUX BERQUIN	4/10.	—	Brigade left NOELLES at 5 a.m. and marched to VIEUX BERQUIN as directed in orders 108/4. March 17 miles. Billeted on outskirts in farms. Weather showery. Condition of horses good.	A.H./. 108/4.
PROVEN	5.10.	—	Marched at 10 a.m. via route in orders 108/4. Billeted Bde. Brigade in farms nearby. Bt-B.Col. E.C.W.D. WALTHALL. D.S.O. took over Command of the Brigade.	108/4. A.H./.
PROVEN.	6.10	—	Brigade inspected by Maj-Gen. J.S. CAPPER. C.B. Cmdg. 24th Divn. 2 Lt. W.J. DEACON and 2 Lt. P. CONDON joined and are posted to C & A Bty's respectively. 2 Lt. W.H. LEWIS posted to A Bty from Bde. Amm. Col. Orders received (108/15) re being attached to IX Division for instruction. Directed by Gen. Capper Cmdg 24th Divn.	A.H./. 108/15.

Army Form C. 2118

3

WAR DIARY

INTELLIGENCE SUMMARY.

Headquarters.
108 Bde R.F.A.

(Erase heading not required.)

Instructions regarding War Diaries and Intelligence Summaries are contained in F. S. Regs., Part II. and the Staff Manual respectively. Title pages will be prepared in manuscript.

Place	Date	Hour	Summary of Events and Information	Remarks and references to Appendices
			Map. Hazebrouck 1:100,000	
	10/15			
PROVEN.	7/10	—	Capt. R.N.V. Montgomery joined and takes over command of "A" Battery. Attached orders (105/6) reinvedre road to new billetting area.	HRJ. 105/6.
BOESCHÈRE	8/10	—	Brigade marched from PROVEN at 9.30 a.m & arrived at 12.30 p.m. Billets 1 mile N.E. of BOESCHÈRE. One section of B/108 went into action beside DICKEBUSCH Étang.	HRJ.
BOESCHÈRE	9/10	—	Remained in billets resting.	HRJ.
BOESCHÈRE	10/10	—	Remaining section of B/108 joined Battery in action beside DICKEBUSCH Étang.	HRJ.
BOESCHÈRE	11/10	—	Brig. Remained in billets.	HRJ.
BOESCHÈRE	12/10	—	Brig. Remained in billets.	HRJ.

Army Form C. 2118

WAR DIARY
INTELLIGENCE SUMMARY.
(Erase heading not required.)

Headquarters.
105 Bde. R.F.A.

Instructions regarding War Diaries and Intelligence Summaries are contained in F. S. Regs., Part II. and the Staff Manual respectively. Title pages will be prepared in manuscript.

Place	Date	Hour	Summary of Events and Information	Remarks and references to Appendices
	1915.		Sheet 28 Belgium.	
BOESCHEPE	13/10	—	Remained in Billets.	AFW
BOESCHEPE	14/10	—	" " "	AFW
BOESCHEPE	15/10	—	One gun of D Bty ordered to take up a position at N 28 B 5.9. To enfilade sunken road 08 D 9.7 to 0 4.8.4. To register works and R.F.C.	AFW
BOESCHEPE	16/10 to 31/10	—	Remained in billets. Horse standings etc are being made by batteries & A.C. Existing billets in camps for men also been improved.	AFW
"	27.10	—	19 NCOs & men under Capt Birch Jarvis a Corporal farrier from the 24th Divn & were inspected by H. M. King George	

J.C. Walthull
Major. R.F.A. o Bgt. H.U.
Comdy. 105 Bde. R.F.A.

"A" Form.   **Army Form**
MESSAGES AND SIGNALS.   No. of Message

Prefix	Code	m.	Words	Charge	This message is on a/c of:	Reed. at ___ m.
Office of Origin and Service Instructions.			Sent			Date
			At ___ m.		___ Service.	From
			To			
			By		(Signature of "Franking Officer.")	By

TO — Cant?

| * Sender's Number. | Day of Month. | In reply to Number | AAA |

Cooks cart driver 1

Total per Brigade 80 personnel
80 horses

Bagage lines of 9th Div Batteries should be reached by 11 A.M. where horses will be left aaa Rations for current day to be carried aaa Rations for subsequent days will be supplied by brigade to which attached. aaa

A cooks cart may accompany each party aaa
Bde commanders will order the return of their parties as soon as they consider that they have gained sufficient knowledge of the system of trench warfare 48 hours or less should suffice
Return to be telephoned from 9 Div RA HQ to this office
108th FA Bde will send a similar party about 9th inst

From BM 24 DA
Place
Time 1 pm

The above may be forwarded as now corrected. (Z) J.R. Hodway

Censor. Signature of Addresser or person authorised to telegraph in his name.

"A" Form.
MESSAGES AND SIGNALS.

Army Form C.

Prefix SM. Code HDP. Words 97 Charge
Office of Origin and Service Instructions
FX

Sent At ___ m. To ___ By ___

This message is on a/c of:
___ Service.
(Signature of "Franking Officer.")

No. of Message
Recd. at 108/6
Date
From 84
By

TO { 108th (How) BRIGADE }

Sender's Number	Day of Month	In reply to Number	AAA
* BM 150	4th		

Reference HAZEBROUK 5 A map AAA Reference BM 149 AAA 108 and 109th FA brigades will march to new billeting areas tomorrow AAA 108th starting point ANN 1 mile N of WATOU 9.30 AM AAA Route via ABEELE — BOESCHEPE AAA Billeting parties to meet Brigade major at BOESCHEPE church at 10.30 AM AAA 109 starting point P of PROVEN 10.30 AM AAA The route via POPERINGHE — REMINGHELST AAA Billeting parties to meet Brigade major at REMINHELST at 11.30 AM. AAA Squared maps will be required by billeting parties. AAA

From	B.M. 24 DA
Place	
Time	7-50 PM

The above may be forwarded as now corrected. (Z)
Censor. Signature of Addressor or person authorised to telegraph in his name.
° This line should be erased if not required.

"A" Form.   Army Form C

MESSAGES AND SIGNALS.   No. of Message

Prefix	Code	m.	Words	Charge	This message is on a/c of	Recd. at	m.
Office of Origin and Service Instructions.			Sent		108 Service	Date	
			At .... m.			From	
			To				
			By		(Signature of "Franking Officer.")	By	

108/5

TO All Brigades 24th Divl Artl & 24th DAC
repeated 24th Div, 9th Divl Art, 5th Corps.

Sender's Number	Day of Month	In reply to Number	AAA
BM 138			

106 107 & 109th (How) FA Bdes will each send the following parties to be attached to FA Brigades of 9th Div. Parties will march at 8 AM tomorrow 9th

Brigade Headquarters	Bde Commander	1	
	Orderly Officer	1	
	Telephonists	8	
	Horse holders	4	
	RSM	1	
Each Battery	Officers	2	
	Telephonists	6	
	Numbers 1	2	
	Horse holders	4	
	NCO for magazine	1	
BAC	Officer	1	
	NCO's & trumpeters	3	

From Exact destination will be notified later.
Place
Time

The above may be forwarded as now corrected.   (Z)

Censor.   Signature of Addresser or person authorised to telegraph in his name.

* This line should be erased if not required.

"A" Form.
MESSAGES AND SIGNALS.

Army Form C. 2121.

Date 10/8/4

TO: Advance Copy for OC 108 Bde RFA

Day of Month: 3rd   AAA

1st Army wires begins Artillery and D.A.C.s of 21st and 24th Divns will march tomorrow Oct. 4th as follows starting at 5 a.m. aaa 21st Division via BETHUNE LOCON LES LOBES MERVILLE to HAZEBROUCK where they will rejoin their Division. AAA 24th Divn by the same route as far as MERVILLE and thence to billets about VIEUX BERQUIN whence they will continue their march on Oct. 5th via ///// CAESTRE STEENVOORDE thence eastward ½ mile thence N E BAVEKOT and thence to WATOU where they will rejoin their Division AAA Officer of 24th Divisional Artillery to proceed in advance to Headquarters 3rd Corps LA MOTTE to arrange billets at VIEUX BERQUIN AAA Ammunition Subpark vehicles of 21st and 24th Divisions still in 1st Army area will proceed tomorrow to STRAZEELE and HAZEBROUCK respectively via the LILLERS AIRE HAZEBROUCK road AAA ends AAA

(2)

waggon lines are changed so that supplies may be sent up

b. S.O.S. Call from Infantry means
    10 min intense fire
    10 min medium „
    10 min slow „
on night lines

7. <u>Returns</u>   The following returns are required daily
(1) at 10 A.M. & 6 p.m.
    Situation & general progress
(2) by 5 p.m.
    Daily casualty report
(3) Ammunition report from 8 p.m. to 8 p.m. to be sent in as soon after 8 p.m. as possible

1st Oct 1915

1. B177
2. 767th
3. 75th
4. 108

Je Pile
Capt R.R.A

Issued at 8.15 p.m.

108/22

Orders by Lt Col Cartwright DSO
Comdg Left Group R.F.A.

1. Brigade Commanders will see their Infantry brigadiers without fail daily

2. Helio & lamp communications back from Battery O.Ps to Battery positions will be arranged.
   Wire will be run along trenches & properly labelled & pinned in or will be dug in.

3. All F.O.O.s will try and locate the following to-morrow morn
   H.20 D.3.4
   A Howitzer battery is going to range on this point with aeroplane observation
   This battery will fire one salvo of 4 guns at 6 p.m. to-morrow night. in order to point out to all F.O.O.s the position of this point
   F.O.O.s to be warned accordingly.

4. Brigades will please notify the O i/c Supplies whenever their

Gen Wardrop wishes your
B. Co to note that this
line is very near the
British line and requires
careful registering

B. ~~A19A41 - H79C55~~

C. (H19C45 - H19C61)

D. H19C62 - H19a66.

(108/3)

To O.C 108th Bde

From Left Group

Kindly arrange to carry
out a Barrage of fire on
same points as last night.
The same rate of fire —
Our Infantry are attempting
to dig a trench from
H 13.09 to H 19 A 0.5. and
want to prevent the Germans
interfering with them.

[signature]
Capt
Bombardier L Group

2 Oct.
4.40 p.m

To O.C. 108th Brigade. R.F.A.

From O.C. Left Group

—

Your brigade will fire on road from H.13.A.4.1. to H.19.A.b.5 to night. as follows:—

One gun will have about 50 yards of front. Fire rounds an hour per gun all night and at irregular intervals. From 6 PM to 6 AM

108th. Brigade Orders
by
Major the Hon. R. Hamilton. R.F.A.   No.20.

56.Move.   Batteries will proceed to Wagon lines and will be clear
           of Gun positions by 12 midnight to-night.
           The Brigade will march to-morrow to VIEUX BERQUIN via
           BETHUNE, LES LOBES and MERVILLE.
           Order of march. Hq. B. C. D Btys and A.C.
           Head of column to be at a point 1 mile N.W. of cross-
           roads in NOYELLES LES VERMELLES on the LENS-BETHUNE
           road facing N.W.
           Billetting parties to report to Adjutant at the head of
           the column at 5 a.m.
           The Brigade will march off at 5 a.m.

In the Field.   Capt.R.F.A.
3/10/15.   Adjutant 108th. Brigade.R.F.A.

108th. Brigade Orders
by
Major the Hon. R. Hamilton. R.F.A.　　　No. 21.

57. Dial Sights and Range finders. A statement showing number and description of Dial sights and range finders in possession of Batteries and A.C. to be rendered at once. This will expedite supply.

58. Guns. etc. All indents for guns etc. must invariably state for what purpose required, i.e. to replace unservicable, to replace loss in at action, damaged in action and as full particulars as possible given.

59. Sergeants. A nominal seniority roll of all Sergeants recommended for promotion is to be submitted without delay. Dates of promotion to be quoted.

60. Guns. Accidents or casualties to guns are to be reported immediately giving full particulars.

61. March. The Brigade will march to WATOU to-morrow. via CASTRE, STEENVORDE and RATTEKOT.
Order of march:- Hq., C, D, B Btys and A.C.
Head of column to be at cross roads 1 mile N.W. of V in VIEUX BERQUIN ready to march off at 10 a.m.
Billetting parties to report to Adjutant at head of column at 10 a.m.

[signature]
Capt. R.F.A.
Adjutant 108th. Brigade R.F.A.

4/10/15.

108th. Brigade Orders
by
Lt.Col. E.C.Walthall.D.S.O.,R.F.A.   No.22.

62. A.V.C. Sergeants. A.F. B.103 are to be sent to the A.D.V.S. 24th. Division without delay. A report showing how these Sergeants are armed is also to be sent to the A.D.V.S.

63. Attachment. All men, horses, vehicles etc. of A Battery now attached to other Batteries will rejoin their own Battery at 9 a.m. to-morrow. Orderlies will report to 2Lt. Hector at C/108 Bty. Hq. at 8 a.m. to be shown where the Battery will reform.

64. Guns. Guns requiring repairs should be taken to 6th. Corps Workshops at PROVEN and Armament Artificers are to accompany them. A report will be rendered to this Office if any guns are being sent to be repaired.

65. Cable and Telephones. Officers Commanding Batteries will render a return to this Office by 10 a.m. to-morrow showing what deficiencies of cable and telephones.
Repairs to telephones will be carried out by O.C. Signals 24th. Division, a notification of work to be executed being sent to that Office before the instrument is sent in.

66. Command. Bt.Lt.Col. E.C.D.Walthall, D.S.O., R.F.A. having being taken on the strength of the Brigade assumes command from this date vice Major the Hon. R.G.A. Hamilton. Master of Belhaven and Stenton. R.F.A. temporarily commanding the Brigade.

Capt.R.F.A.
Adjutant 108th. Brigade R.F.A.

5/10/15.

108th. Brigade Orders
by
Bt.Lt.Col.E.C.Walthall. D.S.O., R.F.A.
                                                            No. 23.

67. Postings. 2Lt. W.H.Lewis is posted to A Battery from the Bde. Amm. Col.
2Lt. W.J.Deacon having been taken on the strength of the Brigade is posted to C Battery.
2Lt. T.Condon having been taken on the strength of the Brigade is posted to A Battery.
2Lt. M.Gliddon will rejoin the Ammunition Column to-morrow.

68. Sick Parade. Sick parade will be at the Headquarters wagon lines at 9 a.m. daily. When the Brigade is in action this parade will take place at an Aid Post the position of which will be notified later.

69. War Diaries. The Unit mentioned in F.S.R. Part 2 refers to the Brigade and not to Batteries.

70. Attachment. Parties as follows will be sent to the 9th. Division for instruction about the 9th. inst.
Hq.   Orderly Officer.   1.
         Telephonists.   8.
         Horseholders.   4.
         R.S.M.   1.
Each Battery.
         Officers.   2.
         Telephonists.   6.
         Horseholders.   4.
         N.C.O for wagon line.   1.
Bde. A.C.
         Officer.   1.
         N.C.Os & Horseholders. 3.
         Cook's cart driver.   1.

71. Roll. The Nominal roll of N.C.Os must be rendered by noon to-morrow. This roll must show whether men are Regulars or not also if recommended for promotion or not and the dates of promotion.

                                          Capt. R.F.A.
                                   Adjutant 108th. Brigade R.F.A.

6/10/15.

108th. Brigade Orders
by
Bt. Lt. Col. E.C. Walthall. R.F.A.

No. 24.

72. Officers.   Capt. R.N.V. MONTGOMERY R.F.A. having joined the Brigade is posted to ~~A Battery~~ command A Battery.

73. Promotions.   No. 64095 Cpl. R.N. Hughes to be Sergeant.
No. 1718 Cpl. R.C. Lester to be Sergeant.
No. 16151 Cpl. B. Williams to be Sergeant.
No. 26773 Br. C. Grady to be Corporal.
No. ------ Br. Butters. C.S. to be Corporal.
No. 9124 Br. P. Wickenden to be Corporal.
No. 1717 @Br. Gr. W. Lester to be Bombadier.
No. 9107 @Br. H.E. Graham to be Bombadier.
all with effect from to-day's date.

74. Postings.   No. 10510 Cpl. F.J. Hawker to B Bty.
No. 68394 Cpl. A. Beavis to Bde. Staff.
No. 13674 Br. J. Davies to A Bty.
No. 9077 Br. J.F. Smith to Bde. Staff.
No. 17270 Gr. W.G. Samways to C Bty.
No. 16666 Gr. Holsworth to Bde. Staff.
No. 1891 Dr. G. Cotton to Bde. A.C.

7/10/15.

Capt. R.F.A.
Adjutant 108th. Brigade R.F.A.

108th. Brigade Orders
by
Lt.Col. E.C.Walthall. D.S.O., R.F.A.

No. 25.

75. Postings.
No.16151 Sgt. B.Williams from D Bty. to A Bty.
No.83192 Gr. Cooper.R. from A.C. to A Bty.
No.85689 Dr. Laws.A. from A Bty. to A.C.
No.67840 Gr. Middleton.F. from A.C. to C Bty.
No.67849 Gr. Hammond.H. from A.C. to C Bty.
No.94906 Gr. Cannell.W. from A.C. to C Bty.
No.86329 Gr. Green.H.A. from A.C. to C Bty.
No.67854 Gr. Richardson. from A.C. to C Bty.
No.85672 Gr. Dobson.A. from A.C. to C Bty.

76. Evacuation of Stores.
It is notified for information of all units that the proper method for evacuation of surplus stores and unservicable stores etc. is as follows (a) Stores are to be sent to refilling point early enough to catch the lorries which will take them to railhead. O. i/c lorries must be asked to arrange it on the spot so as not to block the road. (b) Stores sent back by units in the empty supply wagons will be sent to railhead under arrangements to be made by O.C. Train.

77. Ammunition.
Besides the daily expenditure ammunition returns when operations are in progress involving and continuous and increased expenditure, Batteries are to submit daily at 12.10 p.m. and 8.10 p.m. statements showing approximate amount of ammunition on hand at 12 noon and 8 p.m. respectively. This will also be sent in by the A.C. H.E. and Shrapnel to be shown seperately.

H.S.Wintle Capt.R.F.A.
Adjutant 108th. Brigade R.F.A.

8.10.15.

108th. Brigade Orders
by
Bt.Lt.Col.E.C.Walthall.D.S.O.,R.F.A.

No. 26.

78. Requisitions.	Batteries will requisition on the Bde.A.C. and not on Ordnance for all spare parts and fittings which are carried by the A.C. The A.C. will then fill up from the D.A.C. requisitioning on Ordnance for such articles ONLY as the D.A.C. cannot supply. In future all indents for instruments, wire insulating, tape and other telephone accessories will be sent by Batteries to this Office. A combined indent for the Brigade will be sent in.
79. Ammunition.	Batteries will make every effort at all times to keep filled up with ammunition.
80. Establishment.	The proper establishment of Bombadiers is nine and Paid acting Bombadiers six per Battery, A.C. five Bombadiers and seven Paid acting. Os.C. will please fill up to these numbers.
81. Cashier.	The Field Cashier will be found at ABEELE. (V Corps)

Capt.R.F.A.
Adjutant 108th. Brigade R.F.A.

9/10/15.

108th. Brigade Orders
by
Bt. Lt. Col. E.C. Walthall. D.S.O., R.F.A.

No. 27.

82. Promotions.
No. 80595 @Br. Smith. W. to be Bombadier.
No. 9078 @Br. Remnant. E.J. to be Bombadier.
No. 47006 Gr. Carman. to be Bombadier.
No. 55256 Gr. Coster. E.T. to be Pd. @Br.
No. 10159 Dr. Winterburn. G. to be pd @Br.
No. 102398 Gr. Kebble. W. to be Pd. @Br.
No. 55236 Gr. Pierce. A.E. to be Pd. @Br.

Supplies. 83.
Batteries and A.C. must have a mounted N.C.O. in charge of Supply wagons. Indents to be sent to Brigade Office. A Q.M.S. will be detailed for duty weekly and he will report to the R.S.M. for the indents which he will take with him to the refilling point. He will ask the Supply Officer the assessed weight of the trusses. He will be responsible that they draw up the amount of supplies for which they have indented. If the full amount is not available the Supply Officer must be asked for an explanatory note to be shown to the C.O.

84. Postings.
No. 94996 Gr. Cannel. W. from C/108 to Bde. A.C.
96329 Gr. Green. H. from C/108 to Bde. A.C.

85. Officers' Letters.
Officers letters for the early post should reach this Office by 11 a.m. daily. These letters will be delivered in London the following morning.

86. Fire.
Every precaution must be taken to prevent fire in billets. A receptacle full of dry sand or of earth must be kept in every building in which straw is used for bedding. Some form of fire drill and stations should be improvised and practised in every unit. Naked lights and smoking in barns etc. are prohibited. A useful form of candle lamp can be made from the bottom half of a bottle.

87. Baths.
It is hoped that the Divisional baths in the brewery at BOESCHEPE will be at the disposal of the Brigade one day this week, probably Wednesday, when some of the N.C.Os. and men of the Brigade will be able to get hot baths. Details will be issued later.

Capt. R.F.A.
Adjutant 108th. Brigade R.F.A.

10/10/15.

108th. Brigade Orders.
by
Bt.Lt.Col. E.C.Walthall. D.S.O., R.F.A.

No. 28.

88. Teams. Batteries and Ammunition Column will provide six pairs of horses for wak work under Officer i/c Roads 5th. Corps. Teams should be at POPERINGHE Siding G.T.d. at 8 a.m. on October 12th. 1915. They are required to work full day. They will take swingle trees with them. Feeds for the horses will be taken and also food for the men. The O.C. "A" Battery will detail an Officer to accompany the party which will be formed up on the road between A Battery and 108th. Bde. Hdqrs at 7 a.m. ready to move off.

89. Orders. Attention is called to 24th. Division Routine Orders Nos. 185, and 194.

Capt. R.F.A.
Adjutant 108th. Brigade R.F.A.

11/10/15.

108th. Brigade Orders
by
Bt.Lt.Col. E.C.Walthall. D.S.O., R.F.A.

No. 29.

90. Signalling Stores.	Reference Bde. Order No.78 dated 9/10/15:- Batteries will render a statement to this Office showing all deficiencies in Cable, D.III, telephones etc. These statements are to be strictly accurate. These statements will be compiled and an indent for the Brigade will be submitted. Every unit is supposed to have their full establishment of cable in hand in addition to any cable they have laid out. Statements to be rendered weekly on Wednesdays by 12 noon.
91. Bran.	Bran and linseed cake can be secured locally in exchange for oats. Unit commanders requiring any either of these articles can get them on application to the Brigade Interpreter.
92. Officers.	Second Lieutenants Condon and Deacon will be in attendance at 12 noon to-morrow at R.A. Divisional Headquarters at RENNINGHELST. (First house on the left close to Office of D.A.D.O.S.) To be introduced to G.O.C., R.A.
93. Lecture.	The Commandant Trench Mortar School will give a lecture to-morrow at 4 p.m. at the Divisional Grenade School. Sheet 27.M.10.a.3.9. Os.C. A, C and D Btys and A.C. will attend.
94. Vehicles.	The number of the Division will be painted out on all vehicles.

Capt. R.F.A.
Adjutant 108th. Brigade R.F.A.

12/10/15.

105th. Brigade Orders
by
Bt. Lt. Col. E.C. Walthall. D.S.O., R.F.A.

No. 80.

95. Baths.	The Baths in BOESCHEPE will be available for use as follows to-morrow. Parties will parade at the times stated below at the Baths in the Brewery in BOESCHEPE.

    11 a.m.   Hq. 15 men.
                           Bde. A.C. 45 men.
    12 noon.   B Bty. 30 men.
    1.30 p.m.   A Bty. 35 men.
    2 p.m.   C Bty. 40 men.
    2.45 p.m.   D Bty. 35

Men must take their own soap and towels. A change of underclothing may be obtained if desired. Two Officer's baths are also available at the same times.

96. Stores.	Timber issued for the purpose of making dugouts, gun pits etc, is on no account to be used for fuel. All ranks are to be made acquainted with this order.
97. Promotions.	No. 1804 @Br. Smoothy. S. to be Bombardier. No. 10478 @Br. Fisk. W.R. to be Bombardier. No. 16515 @Br. Matthews. R. to be Bombardier. No. 10911 Gr. Rodgers. A. to be @Br. No. 26261 Dr. Jones. W. to be @Br. No. 1105 Dr. Crook. A. to be @Br. No. 66143 Dr. Rew. F. to be @Br.
98. Transfer.	No. 54773 Sgt. Barnard H. is transferred to B Bty from Amm. Col. No. 28493 Sgt. Coslett. E.R. from B Bty to A.C. No. 47939 Cpl. Secker. W. from A.C. to D Bty. No. 1315 Cpl. Green J. from D Bty to A.C. No. 67870 Br. Thaine. A.R. from A.C. to A Bty. No. ------ Br. Jobling. C. from A Bty. to A.C.
99. Vegetables.	Batteries will not purchase vegetables or requisition vegetables for themselves. The Requisitioning Officer for this group has an ample supply.
100. Cable lines.	Battery Commanders will ensure that they are provided with a sufficiency of distinguishing wood, metal (or of other durable material) tags to affix at not less than each 200x to their telephone lines. Any cables not distinguished may be recovered and used by any unit requiring them. (Leather tags have been found to be very suitable.) Batteries will take steps to make pins for securing their wire in trenches.

101. Furious riding. Complaints have been received from the 5th. Corps of furious riding on the roads. It is hoped that this does not refer to the 24th. Divisional Artillery.

102. Sand bags. There is a large supply of sandbags at the 24th. Div. Artillery Headquarters which will be issued to units on demand.

103. Dandy brushes. Attention is directed to G.R.O. No.449 under which authority is given for the issue of dandy brushes in lieu of horse brushes.

104. Affiliation. Affiliation of R.F.A. Brigades to Infantry Brigades is as follows:-
    106th. Bde. R.F.A. to 73rd. Inf. Bde.
    107th. Bde. R.F.A. to 17th. Inf. Bde.
    108th. Bde. R.F.A. to 72nd. Inf. Bde.

Capt. R.F.A.
Adjutant 108th. Brigade R.F.A.

13/10/15.

108th. Brigade Orders
by
Bt.Lt.Col.E.C.Walthall. D.S.O.,R.F.A.

No. 31.

105. Discipline. Although the march discipline of the Brigade as a whole is good, the O.C. has noticed a good deal of straggling of small parties under junior N.C.Os. Mounted or dismounted, on fatigues, going to hospital, baths, etc, in fact on all occasions all parties are to be properly fallen in and marched to their destination by the N.C.O. in charge. The rules of march discipline are to be as strictly adhered to by small parties as by whole units. This order is to be explained to all N.C.Os.

106. Supply Wagons. The Supply wagons will from to-morrow live with their units, the three extra wagons remaining with Brigade Headquarters. These wagons will proceed to and from the refilling point daily under the B.Q.M.S. on duty and great care is to be taken to ensure punctuallity. The instructions contained in my circular memo on this subject will come into force from Saturday 16th. inst.

107. Officers. Os.C. Batteries and Ammunition Column will report to this Office the names of any Officers who are qualified as:- Architects, Surveyors, Builders, Land agents, Mining Engineers, Experts in explosives.

108. Strength. It is notified for information that men admitted into hospital sick should not be struck off the strength until a notification has been received from Field Ambulance that they have been evacuated to a casualty clearing Station. In the same way, horses admitted to Mobile Veterinary Sections for treatment, should not be struck off until a notification has been received through V.O. in charge that they have been sent away.

109. Claims. Batteries and A.C. will indent for A.F. P.1934A and in future will submit their own claims for allowances. Claims for September have been submitted for all by the Brigade.

Capt.R.F.A.
Adjutant 108th. Brigade R.F.A.

14/10/15.

108th. Brigade Orders
by
Bt.Lt.Col. E.C.Walthall. D.S.O., R.F.A.
No. 82.

110. Punishment. No.10279 Gr. W.A.R.BRAGG, 108th. Bde. R.F.A. was tried by a Field General Court Martial on the following charge:g
"Neglecting to obey Brigade Orders"
The sentence of the court was "To suffer field punishment, that is to say, Field Punishment No.2 for 42 days.

111. Transfer. No.16650 Br. Staples from Hq. to Amm. Col.
No.65851 Br. Sarson.W. from Amm. Col. To Hq.

H.S.Whistle.
Capt. R.F.A.
Adjutant 108th. Brigade R.F.A.

15/10/15.

108th. Brigade R.F.A.
by
Bt.Lt.Col. E.C.Walthall. D.S.O., R.F.A.

No. 88.

112. Divine Service.	Church of England will parade for Divine Service in the field at 108th. Bde. Hdqrs. at 10.30 a.m. to-morrow. Markers will report to the R.S.M. at 10.25 a.m.
113. Teams.	Batteries and Amm. Col. will each detail six pairs of horses for work under Officer i/c Roads, 5th. Corps. A N.C.O. from each Battery and the A.C. will accompany the teams, the senior will take charge. Teams will parade on the road between A Bty. and Hdqrs. ready to move off at 7 a.m. Swingle trees to be taken. Feeds for horses and food for the men will also be taken. The N.C.O. in charge will march the party to POPERINGHE Siding.G.7.d.
114. Orders.	Attention is called to the following orders, 24th. D.R.O. Nos. 245, 249, 254 and 256 d/-15/10/15.

[signature]
Capt. R.F.A.
Adjutant 108th. Brigade R.F.A.

16/10/15.

115. Indents.	Indents for material for making Standings for horses etc. may now be submitted to the C.R.E. These will be sent through the Brigade Office.

108th. Brigade Orders
by
Bt.Lt.Col. E.C.Walthall. D.S.O., R.F.A.

No. 34.

116. Indents. The R.E. will now accept indents for materials for standings etc. These will be submitted by Batteries. Care must be taken that sufficient transport is sent ~~far~~ to take away all that is indented for.
Cement may be ~~drawn~~ drawn but economy must be exercised and when making concrete four parts of sand or rubble must be used with one part of cement. Earth must not be mixed with the cement.

H.S.Whittle
Capt.R.F.A.
Adjutant 108th. Brigade R.F.A.

17/10/15.

108th. Brigade Orders
by
Bt.Lt.Col. E.C.Walthall. D.S.O., R.F.A.

No. 35.

117. Maps. All 1.40,000 and 1.20,000 maps of BETHUNE and neighbourhood should be returned to this Office by 12 noon to-morrow.

118. Horse Standings. etc. The G.O.C. is very anxious that all hutting and other material for standings, roads, etc should be obtained through the C.R.E. He does not want to hamper energetic units in any way, but he wishes to prevent competition in the market, and also to be sure that cover for men is provided before cover for horses. If material for standings can be found the C.R.E. will be open to buy it. Instruction in building wattle and daub huts will be arranged by Hdqrs. 24th. Division. If units wish to avail themselves of this a report will be rendered to this Office stating time etc.

119. Baths. Batteries and A.C. will detail parties as under to parade at the Baths, BOESCHEPE on Friday the 22nd. inst. at the times stated:-

10.30 a.m.	Hq.	20 men.
	B Bty.	40 "
11.30 "	A.C.	50 "
	C Bty.	10 "
2 p.m.	C Bty.	30 "
	D "	30 "
3 "	D Bty.	15 "
	A "	45 "

[signature]

Capt. R.F.A.
Adjutant 108th. Brigade R.F.A.

18/10/15.

108th. Brigade Orders
by
Bt.Lt.Col. E.C.Walthall. D.S.O., R.F.A.

No. 36.

120. Hay nets.	The date on which indents were submitted for hay nets is to be reported by 12 noon to-morrow. They are to be taken into use when received.
121. Orders.	Attention is called to 24th. Division Order No.292 d/-19/10/15. (Tube helmets.)
122. Parade.	Farrier Q.M.Sgts. and A.V.C. Sgts. will parade at the Ammunition Column at 2.30 p.m. every Wednesday until further orders.
123. Reduction.	Under Section 183 (2) of the Army Act, the following are reduced to the ranks:- No.47941 Br.W.Lewis. No.10519 Br.H.Potten.
124. Horses.	It has been noticed that horses have been tethered to trees. This is to be stopped at once.
125. Letters.	All letters wh etc. which have been received for men who have been wounded etc. MUST be signed by an Officer before returning to Bde. Office for posting.
126. Telephones.	Two D III Telephones sent to the Divisional Signal Coy. for repair are now ready and should be sent for to-morrow.

[signature]
Capt. R.F.A.
Adjutant 108th. Brigade R.F.A.

19/10/15.

108th. Brigade Orders
by
Bt.Lt.Col. E.C.Walthall. D.S.O., R.F.A. No.37.

127. Teams. Six teams from each Battery and the A.C. to-morrow to work under the Officer i/c Roads, 5th. Corps. All arrangements to be the same as for last time. (See 108th. Bde. Order No. 113 d/-16/10/15.)

128. Cables. The shape for labels for telephone cables for the 24th. Divisional Artillery is triangular. Batteries will take steps to have these made. The name of the unit is to be clearly stated.

[signature], Capt. R.F.A.
Adjutant 108th. Brigade R.F.A.

21/10/15.

108th. Brigade Orders
by
Bt.Lt.Col. E.C.Walthall. D.S.O., R.F.A.

No. 38.

129.
~~128.~~ Divine Service.
A Church of England Service will be held at Headquarters at 9.30 a.m. to-morrow. Arrangements as for last Sunday. Facilities will be given to R.Cs. to attend a Service at BOESCHEPE at 11.30 a.m. to-morrow.

130.
~~140~~. A.F. B213.
9 a.m.
A.F. B213 will be rendered to this Office by XXXXXXX on Saturdays in future.

H.E.Wurtele.
Capt.R.F.A.
Adjutant 108th. Brigade R.F.A.

23/10/15.

108th. Brigade Orders
by
Bt.Lt.Col. E.C.Walthall. D.S.O., R.F.A.
No.39.

131. Teams.	Six pairs from each Battery and the A.C. will parade to-morrow to work under the Officer i/c Roads, 5th. Corps. All arrangements to be the same as for last time. (See 108th. Brigade Order No.113 d/- 16/1015.) This parade will be at 7 a.m. and the Senior N.C.O. will take charge.	
132. Hutting.	Units are still using hutting material for unauthorized purposes and a considerable amount is being spoilt. Commanding Officers must give their attention to this.	
133. Order.	Attention is called to D.R.O. No.419 d/- 24.10.15. (Loitering.)	
134. Baths.	Men for baths will parade as under:-	

Time.	Unit.	Wednesday.	Thursday.
10.30 a.m.	B.	80.	80.
	A.C.	80.	80.
11.30 a.m.	A.C.	10.	15.
	Hq.	10.	5.
	A.	40.	40.
	B.		
2 p.m.	D.	40.	40.
	C.	20.	20.
3 p.m.	C.	20.	20.

135. Returns. The Ammunition return will in future be made up to 12 noon daily and submitted as soon as possible after that time. A.F. B231 is not required in future.

Capt. R.F.A.
Adjutant 108th. Brigade R.F.A.

26/10/15.

108th. Brigade Orders
by
Bt.Lt.Col. E.C.Walthall. D.S.O., R.F.A.

No.40.

136. Q.M.S.	A Battery will find the Q.M.S. for duty next week.
137. Divine Service.	Parade for Church of England Service will be at 10.30 a.m. to-morrow. Arrangements as for last Sunday.
138. Teams.	Batteries and A.C. will find six pairs of horses for work under the Officer i/c Roads, 5th. Corps to-morrow. All arrangements as for last time. To parade on road by Hq. at 7 a.m. and to be under the charge of the senior N.C.O. present.
139. Tents.	All tents requiring re-staining must be done at once.

Capt. R.F.A.
Adjutant 108th. Brigade R.F.A.

30/10/15.

108th. Brigade Orders
by
Bt.Lt.Col. E.C.Walthall. D.S.O.,R.F.A.

No.41.

140. Trades. Reference D.R.O. No.472 the return required will be rendered to this Office by 6 p.m. 5th. Nov.1915. Nil returns need not be rendered.

141. Court of Enquiry. A court of Enquiry will be held to-morrow at such time as the President may appoint to enquire into the case of absence of No. 67772 Br.Smith. C/108. Br. Smith is at present in the 74th. Field Ambulance at Boeschepe.
President.   Capt. P.Y.Birch. R.A.
Members.   One Subaltern to be detailed by O.C.A/108.
     "   "   "   "   "   " B.A.C.
(Members detailed to report to the President at 10 a.m.)

142. Clippers Horse. The following scale for issue of Clippers, horse and machines for clipping has been approved. Indents should be rendered to Ordnance Officers.
Clippers, horse:- 2% of strength of horses.
Machines, horse clipping, Stewart pattern:-
Battery R.F.A. One.
Bde. Amm. Col. One.
Machines, horse clipping Stewart pattern:-
Spare heads:- Three per machine.
(Authority. G.R.O. 1234 d/-29.10.15.)

Capt.R.F.A.
Adjutant 108th. Brigade R.F.A.

31/10/15.

108 RFA

Vol 7

24

10 8th Adv R 7a.
Vol. 6

24.

108ᵗʰ Bde. R.F.A.
vol: 3

D/
7624

24ᵗʰ Divisions

Nov. 15

art
Ar.

Vol. III
Army Form C. 2118.

WAR DIARY
INTELLIGENCE SUMMARY.
(Erase heading not required.)

Headquarters
108 Bde R.F.A.

Place	Date	Hour	Summary of Events and Information	Remarks and references to Appendices
	1915.		Sheet 28 N.W. Belgium.	
BOESCHÈPE	1.11. to 4.11.	—	Brigade remained in billets. 106 B Bty. B Bty is still in action under O.C. 106 Bde R.F.A. at H.35.c.0.6. C Bty was ordered to occupy a position which they had already prepared at H.19.d.H.R.19.8. 1.25.d.7.8.	H.S.
DICKEBUSCH	5.11.	—	Brigade Hq. moved up to DICKEBUSCH (H.33.b.9.7.)	H.S.
"	5.11.	—	One section of D/108 relieved one section of A/106 at 1.26.d.3.3. One section of B/108 came out of action & returned to their Wagon lines near BOESCHÈPE (being relieved by A/106.	H.S.
"	6.11.	—	The other section of D/108 went into action at 1.26.d.3.3. & the remainder of B/108 was withdrawn & returned to join first section at Wagon lines. All reliefs were carried out after dark. A/108 have not come into action yet owing to their position not being ready.	H.S.

Army Form C. 2118.

WAR DIARY
or
INTELLIGENCE SUMMARY.
(Erase heading not required.)

Instructions regarding War Diaries and Intelligence Summaries are contained in F. S. Regs., Part II. and the Staff Manual respectively. Title pages will be prepared in manuscript.

2

Place	Date	Hour	Summary of Events and Information	Remarks and references to Appendices
DICKEBUSCH	1915 6.11.	(continued)	The Brigade has been detailed to do "counter Battery" work. Three batteries will always be in action & one resting. Battery positions at :- H.36.6.7.9, I.25.d.7.9, <s>H.33.d.9.9</s> I.26.d.2.3. Zones to be covered by Brigade :- Zones 0.4, 5, 6, 7, 9, 10, 11 & 7.6 & d. An aerial mast has been put up at Hqs. & Two wireless operators from the R.F.C. have been attached so that observations fro aeroplanes can be taken.	1st L.
"	8.11	-	A/108 moved up into action at H.36.6.7.7	1st L.
"	9.11	-	2 Lieut E BISHOP. R.F.A joined brigade from 24th Div. A.C. & was posted to B.A.C.	1st L.
"	11.11	-	2 Lieut. O. A. SHEPARD transferred from C/108 to BAC/108 & 2 Lieut E. BISHOP vice versa	1st L.
"	12.11	-	One gunner killed & one gunner wounded A/108 whilst laying telephone cable.	1st L.
"	13.11	-	C/108 heavily shelled from 9.15 a.m. - 3.15 p.m. by two 21 c.m. howitzers. No casualties to personnel who were withdrawn to a flank. Two guns were hit a totally damaged. Battery withdrew during night to its wagon line as position was untenable. Capt & adjt. H.A.S. NURTELE posted to command C/109 & left brigade. Sent C.W.M. NOSWORTHY reserve adjutant (d.g. of appt. 7.11.15) 2 Lieut W.H. LEWIS from A/108 to orderly officer A & D/108 took part at 6.30 p.m. in general attachion scheme on 5th Corps front.	1st L.

Army Form C. 2118.

3

WAR DIARY
or
INTELLIGENCE SUMMARY.

(Erase heading not required.)

Place	Date	Hour	Summary of Events and Information	Remarks and references to Appendices
	1915		Map 28. N.W Belgium	
DICKEBUSH	17-11	—	2/Lt W.M. PERRY joined brigade.	fine
"	18-11	—	Shooting with aeroplane observation done by A & D Btys. Result satisfactory. 2/Lt M. GLIDDON posted to A Bty. 2/Lt W.M. PERRY posted to A.C.	fine
	20-11	—	Shooting with aeroplane observation done by A & D Btys. Wireless signals faulty but attempts made good.	fine
	24-11	—	Section of A & D Btys observed & shelled enemy wagon lines. Result complete.	fine
STEENVOORDE	25-11	—	Guns left the Pits & A & D Btys took over new station their places. Brigade moved at ??? hrs to billets about 1 mile S.S.E. of STEENVOORDE.	Map HAZEBROUCK S.A.
ARNEKE	27-11	—	March resumed. Brigade billeted for the night 27-28. at ARNEKE.	fine

Army Form C. 2118.

WAR DIARY
or
INTELLIGENCE SUMMARY.
(Erase heading not required.)

Instructions regarding War Diaries and Intelligence Summaries are contained in F. S. Regs., Part II. and the Staff Manual respectively. Title pages will be prepared in manuscript.

Place	Date	Hour	Summary of Events and Information	Remarks and references to Appendices
MORINGEM	28-11	—	Brigade moved into rest billets at MORINGHEM, 5 miles W.N.W. of ST OMER.	/ar
MORINEHEM	29. 30		} Remained in billets.	

P.L. Wathall
Lt. Col. R.F.A.
Comdg. 108th Bde. R.F.A.

108 R.F.A
24 4D3
Vol 4

WAR DIARY
INTELLIGENCE SUMMARY

108t Bde O.E.
94/7/76

Army Form C. 2118.

Place	Date	Hour	Summary of Events and Information	Remarks and references to Appendices
MORINGHEM	1915 Dec. 1	—	Brigade ordered to move to ALQUINES on the 3rd.	en.
"	2	—	Col. WALTHALL proceeded on leave. MAJ. R. HAMILTON assumed command of the Brigade.	en.
			M.S.M. 2LT J. SMITH & 2LT J. KING joined the Brigade & were attached to Battery A.C. & B. Battery respectively.	en.
A			Billeting reconnaissance of ALQUINES.	en.
ALQUINES	3	—	Brigade moved its billet at ALQUINES.	en.
	4	—	2LT M. GLIDDON, transferred from A.C. to A Bty.	en.
			2LT W.J. DEACON " " " " B "	en.
			2LT W.M. PERRY " " " " C "	en.
			2LT H.L. WEBBER " " D " to A.C.	en.
			LT F.S. POTTER " A.C./268 R.F.A. to C/107 TM	en.
			R.F.A. with effect from the 2nd.	en.
			2LT E.R.F. BOND transferred from C/107 TM. Rifle R.F.A. to A.C./108 Rifle R.F.A. with effect from the 2nd.	en.

Army Form C. 2118.

WAR DIARY
or
INTELLIGENCE SUMMARY.
(Erase heading not required.)

Instructions regarding War Diaries and Intelligence Summaries are contained in F. S. Regs., Part II. and the Staff Manual respectively. Title pages will be prepared in manuscript.

Place	Date	Hour	Summary of Events and Information	Remarks and references to Appendices
ALQUINES.	Dec 5	—	No. 10291 2R.S.M. MARTIN promoted 2/Lt. with effect from 20-11-15 and is struck off the strength.	—
"	5-14	—	Remained in billets.	—
"	14.	—	2/Lt. M.S.M. SMITH posted from A.C. to C battery.	—
"	15.	—	Capt. B.B. GILPIN joined the brigade and was posted to A.C.	—
"	16	—	Remained in billets.	—
"	17	—	Brigade inspected by General Sir H.C.O PLUMER commanding 2nd Army.	—
"	18-31st	—	Remained in billets.	—

F.L. Wrottesley
Lt. 1st A.F.A.

(nearly 1st A.F.A.)

Ishihorde: R.H.
Vol. 5
Pam '16

245

Army Form C. 2118.

WAR DIARY
or
INTELLIGENCE SUMMARY.
(Erase heading not required.)

108ᵗʰ Bde. R.F.A.

Off. STOMER 7 mft 1 / 40,000

Place	Date	Hour	Summary of Events and Information	Remarks and references to Appendices
ALQUINES	1915 Janʸ 1-4ᵗʰ	—	Remained in billets	/ar/
" "	5ᵗʰ	—	Marched to QUELMES	/ar/
QUELMES	6ᵗʰ & 7ᵗʰ	"	Remained in billets.	/ar/
"	8ᵗʰ	"	Marched to NOORDPEENE.	/ar/
NOORDPEENE	9ᵗʰ	"	Marched to STEENWOORDE.	Stor
STEENWOORDE	10ᵗʰ	—	B & C batteries, one section each of A & D batteries, moved up into wagon lines vacated by 80ᵗʰ Bde R.F.A. Ref. 1/40,000 map. Belgium & France Sheet 28.	/ar/
"	11ᵗʰ		In the evening one section each of A, B & D batteries (personnel only) moved up into action in relieve of A, B & E batteries 80ᵗʰ Bde. R.F.A., guns being exchanged. Respective positions being A. I 27 b 3.6. "B" (one section only) I 15 b 2.3. "D" I 14 b 5.6. 2ⁿᵈ sections of A & D batteries. And lot. & H.Q moved up to wagon lines of 80ᵗʰ Bde R.F.A. In the evening & 2ⁿᵈ sections of A & D & H.Q 2 H.Q moved up into action 2 or where being completed. Lt. Col. Walthall assumed Command of Right group of arty. covering Rt Sector of front held by 24ᵗʰ Divn. (72ⁿᵈ Inf. Bde.) with H.Q at I 15 d 1.1	/ar/
ZILLEBEKE LAKE	15ᵗʰ & 16ᵗʰ		This group consists of A, B (12cc) D, 108ᵗʰ Bde. A, 106 Bde & B, 107 Bde. 73ʳᵈ Indy. Bde relieved 72ⁿᵈ Indy. Bde in Rt Sector.	/ar/
	17ᵗʰ	—	Howr. group taken up & B. 109 Bde. & 6ᵗʰ Siege battery were added to Ang. at group.	/ar/

Army Form C. 2118.

WAR DIARY
or
INTELLIGENCE SUMMARY.
(Erase heading not required.)

Place	Date	Hour	Summary of Events and Information	Remarks and references to Appendices
"	19th	—	2nd Lieut. G.W. SHEPARD "D" Battery wounded, slightly in foot.	P/ww
ZILLEBEKE	22nd	—	2nd Section of "B" Battery came up into action joining "A" Battery	P/ww
"	23rd	—	B.107 Bde. withdrawn from group.	P/ww
"	27th	—	A single gun of "C" Battery brought into action near MARIE LOOSE I.24.d.5.9.	P/ww
"	31st	—	O.C. 2 Hd Qrs. relieved in command of Right group by O.C. = H.Q. 105th Bde, & went to billets in POPERINGHE. 1st Section "C" Battery relieved 1st Section "D" Battery in action.	P/ww

P.S. Wadltham
Lt. Col. R.F.A
Commdg. 108th Bde. R.F.A.

Army Form C. 2118.

WAR DIARY
or
INTELLIGENCE SUMMARY.
(Erase heading not required.)

108th Bde. R.F.A.

Ref Sheet 28

Place	Date	Hour	Summary of Events and Information	Remarks and references to Appendices
POPERINGHE	1914 Feb 1st	—	2nd Section "C" battery relieved 2nd Section "D" battery. "D" battery took over the single gun.	R.A.S.
"	7th	—	2nd Lieut M.S.M. SMITH posted to "D" vice T/2/Lt A.W. SHEPARD invalided.	R.A.S.
"	16th	—	H.Q. proceeded to ZILLEBEKE BUND in relief of 109th Bde 2 Lieut.Col. WAITHALL assumed command of Right Group.	R.A.S.
"	—			
YPRES	23rd	—	H.Q. moved to YPRES Ramparts as the BUND had been shelled heavily, many casualties.	R.W.
"	24th	—	"D" battery form not went into action I.24 central 2 howzrs under tactical control of 17th Divn. A single gun belonging to 05/107 in actn at I.3d.7.5— to enfilade trenches at HOOGE journed the single gun regaining its own battery. A single gun belonging to the group 2 was attached to A/106 Bde. under control of the group 2 was attached to A/106 Bde. N.B. Right group now becomes Left group, VI th Divn coming in on our left.	Sect.

P.C. Waithall
Lt. Col. R.F.A.
Comdg 108th Bde. R.F.A.

Army Form C. 2118.

WAR DIARY
INTELLIGENCE SUMMARY

108th Bde. R.F.A.

Ref Sheets 27 & 28

Place	Date	Hour	Summary of Events and Information	Remarks and references to Appendices
YPRES	1916 March 2		2nd Lieut. E.R.P. BOND to orderly officer vice 2nd Lt. W.H. LEWIS to B.A.C.	P.W.
"	4		H.Q. relieved by H.Q. 109th Bde in left group. Moved to billets in POPERINGHE. T/2 Lt A.S. HENDERSON posted to Bde pending absorption. (20.2.16)	P.W.
POPERINGHE	10		H.Q. relieved H.Q. 109th Bde in command of left group. T/2 Lieut W.K. MITCHELL (9.3.16) T/2 Lieuts T.T. RADMORE & J.C. DEW joined Brigade pending absorption.	Sch.
YPRES	14 } 15 }		H.Q. relieved by H.Q. 106th Bde in Left Group. Moved to billets in POPERINGHE. 1 Section "D" battery withdrawn & went to rest in wagon line. (14.3.'16)	P.W.
POPERINGHE	16		Section "D" battery relieved section "B" battery in action, with "A" battery at BLAUWPOORT FARM.	P.W.
	17 } 18 }		Batteries in action (A,B & C) relieved by LAHORE. Div Arty on section each night. "D" battery section in SANCTUARY WOOD relieved by 50th Div: Arty. Batteries as relieved marched by sections to Rest Area between STEENWOORDE & EECKE. (Sheet 27)	P.W. P.W.
EECKE	19	—	Whole Brigade assembled in Rest Area.	P.W.
"	31	—	1 Section each A.B.C. & D batteries; 2½ B.A.C. moved up to new area, 2 in actions in the evening relieving 3rd Bde. Can: F.A. 1st Can: Div.	P.W.

P.J. Bradstreet H/Lt Col R.F.A.
Comdg 108th Bde R.F.A.

WAR DIARY
or
INTELLIGENCE SUMMARY.
(Erase heading not required.)

Army Form C. 2118.

Vol. 8.
108th Bde R.F.A. Ref. Photos 27-28.

Place	Date	Hour	Summary of Events and Information	Remarks and references to Appendices
EECKE	April 1st		2nd Sections A.B.C & D Batteries came up into action & remainder of B.A.C. Hd. Qrs. both arrived from 3rd Can. F.A. Brigade completed 9.30 p.m. We are supporting 72nd Infy. Bde. on left sector of Divl. front V1a 1.8 - N30c 5.5. Positions of batteries:- A. N.24 d. 8.3. "B" (definite battery) T.24 a. 2.9. "C" N.33 a. 8.1. "D". T.3 t.65. H.Q. T.3 a. 2.8. B.A.C. S.5 t. 9.5. 2 Lieuts (R.) BEAL (SR) & W. BEART (Temp) joined the Bde & were posted to C & D batteries	
DRANOUTRE	3rd		2 Lieut. A.G.C. NORTHCROFT struck off strength of Brigade (sick at home). Lt. Col. F.E. WALTHALL resumed command of Bde 2 Major H.O. O'GAHAMPTON assumed command of Bde.	
"	8th		H.Q. Hay hump. Mullet. moved to T. 1 & 6.0.	
"	15th		2nd Lt. A.E. HENDERSON struck off strength. (sent home sick)	
"	20th		Lt Col WALTHALL resumed command.	
"	29th	2 a.m.	Ger. Gas attack on 72nd Infy Bde front. Bde. assisted in repelling it.	

F.E. Walthall
Lt. Col. R.F.A.
Cmndg 108 Bde R.F.A.

WAR DIARY
INTELLIGENCE SUMMARY. 108th Bde. R.F.A. Ref Part 28

Vol. 9
Army Form C. 2118
XXIV

Place	Date 1916 May	Hour	Summary of Events and Information	Remarks and references to Appendices
DRAMOUTRE	6		Establishment of Batteries increased to 5 officers. Following postings in emergency Arty. 2nd ag. O.c.d. A/108 – 2/Lt. W.C. Mitchell. B – 2/Lt. R. Beard. C – 2/Lt. T.F. Andrews. D – 2/Lt. W.H. Jeavons.	Past.
			2/Lt. J.C. Dutt to B.A.C. for Supernumerary	Past.
	4		H.Qrs moved into village of DRAMOUTRE	
	13		Establishment of Brigade changed. D/108 Howrs C/109 B/109/4.5" Horj. becomes D/108. B.A.C. becomes No 3 section D.A.C.	
			Officers struck off strength. Major C.B. Gilpin. Lt. H.L. Holter. 2/Lt. O.H. Shepherd (B.A.C.) Capt. O.J. Burch. Lieut. L.O. Spoor. 2/Lt. W.J. Deacon. 2/Lt. W.H. Jeavons. 2/Lt. M.S.R. Smith (D/108) Officers taken on strength. Capt. O. Hart. Lieut. H. Hatchley. D/ St.Albans. H. Mitton. 2/Lts J.S. Trant. 2/Lt. J.C. Drew Reverts Supernumerary to Estab. 2/Lt. J. Denniston. (Infantry) (B/108)	Past.
	17		Notification received that the Military Medal had been awarded to No. 30123 Gr. D. McAllum No. 31863 Gr. M. McCrann (A/108) & No. 67923 Gr. G.W. Martin (C/109 late D/108) for their gallantry during gas attack on night 30 April.	Past.
	26		Position of Hqrs D/108 battery to T.18.C.88 a Crown whole zone 2/Lt. V.B. Drewitt (S.A.) Joined the Brigade is attached to A battery.	Past. Past.

Army Form C. 2118.

2

Old Sheet 28

WAR DIARY
or
INTELLIGENCE SUMMARY. 108 Bde. R.F.A.

(Erase heading not required.)

Instructions regarding War Diaries and Intelligence Summaries are contained in F. S. Regs., Part II. and the Staff Manual respectively. Title pages will be prepared in manuscript.

Place	Date	Hour	Summary of Events and Information	Remarks and references to Appendices
DONNOITRE	28		2nd Lieut. T. LONDON. A battery accidentally killed. Buried on 29th in DONNOITRE military cemetery. M.35.d.7.7 by Rev. T. Brown C.F.(O.C). 2 Lieut. W. BEART attached in A battery.	Pro- ceed.
"	30		2 Lieut. V.C. DARRINGTON wounded (shell).	

P.V. Wellham
Lt. Col. R.F.A.
Comdg. 108 Bde. R.F.A.

XVV v 10

WAR DIARY
or
INTELLIGENCE SUMMARY.

Army Form C. 2118.

108 Bde. R.F.A.

Part 2?

(Erase heading not required.)

Place	Date	Hour	Summary of Events and Information	Remarks and references to Appendices
DRANOUTRE	1916 June 3		Lieut. L.M. HARVEY C/108 attacked Military Cross. 9077 Cpl. G.F. Burke (H.Q.) Artillery Posted Tom.Coy 2/6/16. 2nd Lieut. J.S. TEAGUE D/108. awarded M.Cross.	P/15.
"	6		2/Lt. N.G. DARRINGTON returned to duty	P/15.
"	17	12.30 a.m.	Heavy gas attack on front of Division but no infantry attack followed. 108 Bde. Ammunition "Gite".	P/15
"	18		2/Lt. W.C. MITCHELL (A/108) 2 Lt. O.O. (B/108) gassed on 17th (Chlorine Cases)	P/15
"	28		No. 34293 G.S.M. H. SPOOR promoted 2nd Lieutenant & posted to 3rd Divn.	P/15.
"	29/25		Group from part in a successful raid carried out by D. Queen's 172nd Infy Bde.	P/15

P.I. Walthall
Lt. Col. R.F.A.

WAR DIARY or INTELLIGENCE SUMMARY

Army Form C. 2118

108 Bde. R.F.A.

Ref Sheet 28 Vol 11

Place	Date 1916 July	Hour	Summary of Events and Information	Remarks and references to Appendices
DRANOUTRE	1st		2nd Lieut. V.G. DARRINGTON wounded in A/108 via 2nd Lieut. W.C. MITCHELL wounded.	
"	"		26th Brit. 7th Australian Bde. relieved 1st Bde. of 72nd Rfy. Bde. & are covered by 108 Bde. group.	
"	4/5		B/108 → D/108 1st Section relieved by 14 × 105 Australian Howitzer respectively. Sections sideshow to respective posn.	
"	5/6		2nd Section B → D/108 relieved & withdrew to wagon line. 1st Section C/109 relieved by 10th Aust. 2 Battery & withdrew to its wagon line.	
"	6/7		2nd Section C/109 relieved & withdrew to wagon line. 1st Section B/108 relieved A/253 in action at N27 c 8.3.3. C/108 passes under command of O.C. 4 Aust. Bde. R.F.A.	
"	7/8		2nd Section B/108 relieved A/253 in action.	
"	8		Capt. G.A. CAMMELL struck off, invalided. 4th m. 108 Bde. group consists of A=B/102. B/109. D/107. D/108 relieved 105th Aust. 2 Battery in action. C/109 relieved 10th Aust. 2 Battery 1st m. 4th Austin Bde. relieved & hands over command of C/108 C/109 → D/108 to O.C. 108 Bde. group which now consists of 7 batteries. Covers front of 17th Infy. Bde.	
"	9		Casualties – 1 Serg. Killed. 12 Aug. & 3 O.R. wounded. (B/108)	
"	10/11		A/109 occupies position formerly occupied by B/108 & passes into 108 Bde group. (8 batteries) Fresh 4th m. just in successful raid carried out by 3rd Rifle Bde. on enemy's trenches N36a 5.9.	
"	11		4th m. C/108 C/109 D/108 form bde CENTRE GROUP. 1107th Bde.	

Army Form C. 2118.

WAR DIARY
or
INTELLIGENCE SUMMARY.
(Erase heading not required.)

Sheet 28 S.W
" 27
Sheet 17 (AMIENS)

Place	Date	Hour	Summary of Events and Information	Remarks and references to Appendices
DRANOUTRE	July 11.		Group now consists of A/108 [N.36 b 7.10] B/108 [N.27 d 3/9 3/9] A/109 [T 24 c 2½.9] D/107 [N.21 c.8.7] with single gun at T.5.c 3.8.) 2 B/109 [N.34 a 7.2] covering 17 2nd Infy. Bde front. N.36 a 7.2 (WOLVERGHEM - WYTSCHAETE road) to N.30 a 57 (PECKHAM). C/108 (N.33 a 8.1) & D/108 (T.18 c 8.8) are under tactical control of 107th Bde. 2Lieut. F.W.P.DOUGLAS joined 2 i/c attached to D/108. 2Lieut. E. BISHOP (C/108) slightly wounded (shell) 2 remained at duty.	P.W.
"	12.		1 Sec A/109 went out of action to rest. Group front in successful raid on enemy's trenches carried out by 12th Division on N.30.c.17. Arnd.	P.W. P.W.
"	13/14			P.W.
"	17/18		161st July Bde relieved 17th Bgd Bde. a 108 Bde group passed under command of 50th Divn.	P.W. P.W.
"	19/20		Bde Group relieved by 173rd Bde. & moved to rest area near EECKE (Sheet 27) where Brigades came under their own commanders.	P.W.
"	22/23		2Lieut. F.W.P.DOUGLAS joined to B/108. 2Lieut. J.C. DEW marched off Strength, sick.	P.W.
EECKE	23.		Bde entrained, Batteries at GODEWAERSWELDE, HQ at BAILLEUL & proceeded to Battery SALEUX H.Q. LONGUEAU (Sheet 17 1/100,000). Detrained & proceeded by march route to COISY where Bde is concentrated.	
"	26.			P.W.

Army Form C. 2118.

WAR DIARY
or
INTELLIGENCE SUMMARY.
(Erase heading not required.)

Place	Date	Hour	Summary of Events and Information	Remarks and references to Appendices
CROUY	1916 July 29 - 31		2 Sect. E.A.C., Q.A.H.Q., D.L.A. joined the brigade & attached to B/108. Brigade proceeded by march route to VECQUEMONT & DAOURS (M.6 = 12), leaving at 1.30 p.m. arriving 8.10 p.m.	p/ur p/ur

P.L. Holthall
Lt. Col. R.F.A.
Comdg. 108 Bde. R.F.A.

24th Divisional Artillery.

108th BRIGADE

ROYAL FIELD ARTILLERY

AUGUST 1 9 1 6

Army Form C. 2118.

108 Bde. R.F.A. O4 Sheet 17 1/10,000 AMIENS
Sht 62d 1/40,000
62.c.5
57c

Vol 12

WAR DIARY
or
INTELLIGENCE SUMMARY.
(Erase heading not required.)

Instructions regarding War Diaries and Intelligence Summaries are contained in F. S. Regs., Part II. and the Staff Manual respectively. Title pages will be prepared in manuscript.

Place	Date	Hour	Summary of Events and Information	Remarks and references to Appendices
	1916 August			
DAOURS	4th		BRIGADE proceeded by march route, halting 3a.x, to BOIS DES TAILLES.	Plot.
BOIS-DES-TAILLES.	11th	—	1st Section of Batteries went up into action, relieving corresponding batteries of 157 Brigade. R.F.A. A. B = C. A. 3. d. 6.5 - 6.7 (Sht. 62 C). D. A.10.a.6.4.	"
			2ⁿᵈ Lieut. R. BEALE (B)/108 transferred to Z/24. T. M. Battery in relief of 2ⁿᵈ Lt. J.H. SNOWBALL.	Plot.
A.2.d.7½.6½ (62.c)	12th	9a.m.	2ⁿᵈ Sections of Batteries went up into action relieving batteries as above. H.Qrs. relieved H.Qrs. 157 Bde. R.F.A. A.2.d.7½.6½; front covered (Sht 57c) S.30.b.9½.7 - S.24.d.9.3. Held by 72ⁿᵈ Inf. Bde.	Plot.
"	13		Capt/a R. N. MONTGOMERY (A) 2 Lt. H.J. WILKINS (B) wounded (shell). 2ⁿᵈ Lt. G.V.C. SELWYN to see D.A.C. joined.	Plot.
"	22ⁿᵈ 24		2ⁿᵈ Lieut. E.A.G. RAHBULA wounded (slightly, remaining at duty) 2ⁿᵈ Lieut. F.W.Q. DOUGLAS wounded.	Plot. Plot.
"	26ᵗʰ		Brigade has taken part in bombardments & various attacks on GUILLEMONT by the 24ᵗʰ Divⁿ 22/23. 20ᵗʰ Bde. Infy. relieved 24ᵗʰ Inf. Bde. 2ⁿᵈ Lieut. W. DUNNING joined, attached B)/108	Plot. Plot.
"	27ᵗʰ		Lieut. E.S. HECTOR A Batty. to hospital. Lieut W.C. MASKELL A)/106. To Lieutenant A)/108. P.J. Waltham Lt.Col. R.F.A. Comdg. 108 Bde. R.F.A.	Plot.

Royal Artillery

24th Division.

108th BRIGADE R. F. A.

S E P T E M B E R   1 9 1 6

WAR DIARY
or
INTELLIGENCE SUMMARY

Army Form C. 2118.

Ref. Sheet 57c
62c
62d 1/40,000

108 Bde R.F.A.

Vol 13

Place	Date	Hour	Summary of Events and Information	Remarks and references to Appendices
Sut 62c.	Sept 1916			
A 2 d 7½ 6½	1st		2nd Lieut C.R. BOYTON joined on promotion from B.S.M. attached to A.	Air
"	2nd		Lieut T.W. MURRAY joined from 38th Div Arty to command A/108 Lieut W.C. MASKELL returned to A/106	Bir
"	3rd–4th		Brigade took part in attack on GUILLEMONT & GINCHY. In support of 59th Bde 20th Div attacking Southern half of GUILLEMONT. Ordinary trenchment bombardment from 3rd. Attack started at 12 noon on 4th for portion of attack occupied. 2nd Lieut J.S. TEAGUE D/108 x wounded (1st Sept). 2nd Lieut C.R. BOYTON attached to D x (Remaining at duty)	Cir Pair
"	5th		1st Section 76 Bde R.F.A. (Guards Div.) returned 1st Section 108 Bde in return	Pair Pair
"	6th		2nd " " " " " Brigade	
"			Withdrew & marched to rest camp at BOIS des TAILLES; 2 mile August 11, in addition to officer given above the following casualties have occurred. Killed 2 O.R. Missing 1 O.R. Wounded 18 O.R.	Pair Pair
Bois des TAILLES	8th		2nd Lt W. DUNNING transferred to 24th D.A.C. Brigade marched to new wagon lines 62d, F 23.b, with a view to moving up into action	Pair
"	11th		2nd Lt W.C. BLACKIE joined & posted to C. 2nd Lt ... joined & attached to C.	Pair
F. 23.b.	12th		2nd Lt W.B. STEWART joined & posted to C. D battery moved up into action at 57.c. S 30.c.14 & formed under command of O.C. 109 Bde.	Bir

WAR DIARY
or
INTELLIGENCE SUMMARY.
(Erase heading not required.)

Army Form C. 2118.

108 Bde R.F.A.

By. Post 37e

Place	Date 1916 Sept.	Hour	Summary of Events and Information	Remarks and references to Appendices
F.23.d.	13/14		Remainder of brigade moved up into action in support of 71st Infy Bde 6th Divn H.Qrs S 30 b.1.3. A=B T.23a.3.6. C T.23a.1.9. (Bde. took part in attack on MORVAL-LESBOEUFS by 6th Divn. General Bremer 2/Lt J.H. SNOWBALL (A battery) killed in action	Ref
S.30 b.1.3.	15.		D/108 returned to brigade in action at S.30.d.1.4.	Ref
"	16.		Operations continued.	
"	17.		2/Lieuts W.J. BENNETT (A) 2 D.H.S NICHOLSON (B) joined.	Ref
"	18.		QUADRILATERAL taken by 18th & 16th Infy Bdes. 108 Bde in support of 18th G.B.	Ref
"	20/21st		Batteries moved forward. A=B to T.20.a.7.3. D to T.20.c.2.8. in support of 18th G.B. (5th Divn.) who then relieved 18th G.B. C battery to wagon line in reserve having guns derelict between A + B.	Ref Ref
"	21st		H.Q. moved up to GUILLEMONT. T.23a.7.9½	Ref
T.25a.7.9½	22nd		Bde. grouped with 30th Bde. (6th Divn) 2.92nd Bde (20th Divn) in support of 18th Infy Bde. who held line T.9.6.2 to T.3.d.4.1 group commanded by O.C. 108 Bde. Movement forward carried out in very bad weather & under great difficulties Inf: took very few casualties.	Ref
"	24		Bde. took part in attack on LES BOEUFS 2 MORVAL in support of 6th Divn.	Ref
"	25.		2 in division took 18th Infy Bde. Ordinary bombardment 24 + 25. attack at	

Army Form C. 2118.

WAR DIARY
or
INTELLIGENCE SUMMARY.

LENS 11. 3
108 Bde. R.F.a. Ref Sheet 57 C

(Erase heading not required.)

Place	Date	Hour	Summary of Events and Information	Remarks and references to Appendices
1916 Sept.				
T2804.7½	25		Nihil at 12-35 p.m. Completely successful.	Pres.
"	26		Barrage fire during 2 night to cover consolidation of line taken.	Pres.
"	27		1st Jackson's 14th Bde. R.F.a. 4 Bn. relieved 1st Nicholson 108 Bde. in action.	Pres.
"	28		2nd " " " " " " 2 " " " " Q.H.Q.	
			14th Bde. relieved H.Q. 108 Bde. Bde. marched to Bois des TAILLES. During the period 14th–28th the following casualties were reported. Killed 1 O.R. Wounded 1.0R. Missing 1.0R. Wounded 1.12	Pres.
Bois des TAILLES	29		Bde. marched to TALMAS. 2/Lt. V.C. DAGGINGTON (A) accidentally injured, broken thigh. Left from Amiens. 2/Lt. D.H.S. NICHOLSON transferred B to A	Pres.
TALMAS	30		Bde. marched to BRETEL via DOULLENS	Pres.
Just N. LENS				
BRETEL	1st oct.		Orders to standard time. Bde. marched to ORANGEMONT.	—
ORANGEMONT	2nd		Bde. marched to CAMP	Pres.

P.L. Bradwell
Lt. R.F.a
Comdg. 108 Bde. R.F.a.

Nominal Roll of Officers of 108th.Brigade R.F.A. by Batteries

HEADQUARTERS

Lt.Col.E.C.Walthall. D.S.O.
Lieut.C.N.Nosworthy.
2/Lt.W.Beart.

"A" Battery

Maj:Hon:R.G.A.Hamilton.
Capt.P.Y.Birch.
2/Lt.E.Bishop.
2/Lt.W.M.Perry.
2/Lt.T.T.Radmore.

"B" Battery

Capt.L.M.Harvey.
Capt.T.W.Murray.
Lieut.J.Lipschitz.
2/Lt.S.J.King.
2/Lt.M.Gliddon.

"C" Battery

Maj:T.Ryder.
Lieut.W.C.Fairer.
Lieut.W.R.H.Walker.
Lieut.R.C.Couldrey.
2/Lt.A.R.Whitworth.

"D" Battery

Capt.O.Hart.
Lieut.A.S.Bellingham.
2/Lt.J.S.Teare.
2/Lt.E.R.P.Bond.
2/Lt.L.B.Saunders.

ATTACHED

Lieut.J.G.Dutton.
Lieut.E.S.Hector.
Lieut.D.Stalker.
Lieut.C.D.D.Swain.
2/LT.E.A.R.Rahbula.

2/Lt.G.V.S.Selwyn.
2/Lt.D.H.S.Nicholson.
2/Lt.W.B.Stewart.
2/Lt.C.R.Boyton.

Lt.Col.R.F.A.
Comdg.108th.Brigade R.F.A.

Appendix (1)

Vol 14

WAR DIARY
or
INTELLIGENCE SUMMARY. 108 Bde. R.F.A.

Army Form C. 2118.

Sheet 11: LENS.
Sheet 36 B S.E., C S.W.

Place	Date	Hour	Summary of Events and Information	Remarks and references to Appendices
BOETEL	Oct. 1 1916		Return to standard time. Brigade marched to BLANGERMONT	
BLANGERMONT	2		Brigade marched to CAMBLAIN-CHÂTELAIN.	
CAMBLAIN CHÂTELAIN	3		Brigade marched to VERDREL. Reorganized into 2. 6 gun 18 pdr. Batteries & 1. 4 gun Howr. Battery. R.X.A. Battery transferred to C. LX.A. transferred to C. First sections B.&D. made up into action in relief of B.A.2.D. 50th Bde.	
VERDREL	4		H.Q. relieved H.Q. 50th Bde. in BOIS de la HAIE. Remaining sections B.C.D. relieved remaining sections 50th Bde. O.C. 108 Bde. assumes command of Left Group 24th Divn. covering front held by 73rd Infy. Bde. 1 Left Bde. 24th Divn. IV Corps. CARENCY SECTOR. S.15.a.16 to SOUCHEZ river S.3.c.0.5. H.Q 108 Bde. 2 left group X.7.d.1.1. C/108 4 guns X.22.b 02.95. 2 guns X.16.c. 28.45. B/108 2 guns X.16.c. 23.45. 4 guns X.16.c. 15.50. D/108. X.22.a. 94.72. 107 Bde. H.Q. X.26.5.3. 12 18 pdrs. 24 Hows. Dividing line between Bdes. S.9.c.0.P.	
X.7.d.1.1.	7		W. Group took part in raid by 2nd Leinsters.	
" "	8		D/108 detached to 37th Divn. 2 Lieut. 4 gun How. Battery (A/108) arrived from England & relieved D/108 in action.	
" "	10		3 a.r. Group took part in raid by 7th Northants. 17th Infy. Bde. relieved 73rd Infy. Bde. Nominal roll of officers of Bde. as now constituted attached	

Army Form C. 2118.

Ref. Sheet 36. B.S.E.
" C.S.W.

WAR DIARY
or
INTELLIGENCE SUMMARY. 108 Bde. R.F.A.
(Erase heading not required.)

Place	Date 1916 Oct.	Hour	Summary of Events and Information	Remarks and references to Appendices
X 7d.1.1.	13.	—	C battery turned A battery. New howitzer battery named C battery	Mar.
"	17.	—	2nd Lieut. W. G. BLACKIE posted to 32nd Div. A.F. 2 March off	P.M.
"	23.	—	Head Qrs. of Bde. moved to VILLERS-AU-BOIS	
VILLERS AU BOIS	23.	—	Major C. E. Walker ~~posted from 1/24 Div. Art. as supernumary of establishment~~ Sent A.S. BELLINGHAM posted from O.D.C. to R.B.D. 24 Dr. A. 8 posted to D battery Major from 14/24 Bde. (105 Bde. arriving at VILLERS AU BOIS)	Att. P.M.
"	27.	—	2nd Lieut. W. J. BENNETT posted to 1/24 T.M. Battery on a/cmt. & D. D. SWAIN posted to 108 Bde. Lieut. H. MITTON posted to 40 Div. A/y	P.M. P.M.
"	28.	10.42	1 Sm. Dr. (Low estly) took over from 24 Div. (Low estly). Left group now supports 1st Lm. Inf. Bde.	

P. Bratthall.
Lt. Col. R.F.A.
Comdg. 108 Bde. R.F.A.

Army Form C. 2118.

WAR DIARY
or
INTELLIGENCE SUMMARY.
(Erase heading not required.)

Hd Qrs 108 Bde R.F.A.   Sheet 36.O.S.E 2.C.S.W   80/15

Place	Date	Hour	Summary of Events and Information	Remarks and references to Appendices
VILLERS au BOIS	1916 Nov. 5.		2 Lieut. E.A.R. RAHBULA & C.V.S. SELWYN posted to LAHORE DIV. A.C.	Stat.
"	7.		Lieut. W.R.H. WALKER posted to 5th Div a/y. 2 Lieut. C.R. BOYTON attached to C/108	PJat.
"	12.		2 Lt. E.B. Stewart ptd to Wireless Trench Mortars 24th D.A.	-
"	15.		Lieut. W.R.H. WALKER reported to Bde.	Stat.
"	25.		Capt. O.Y. BIRCH transferred to 1st Lpn H.Arty. Lieut. A.S. BELLINGHAM transferred to A/108 as 2nd in command. Lieut. W.R.H. WALKER posted to D/108.	Stat.
"	26.		2 Lieuts. E.S. HECTOR & D. STALKER struck off strength with sick in England. 26/11	Stat.
"	28.		Major Hon. R.G.A. HAMILTON to England with Branch eff.	Stat.
"	29.		Lieut. H. MITTON posted to Brigade from 40th D.A. & attached to D/108	Stat.

C.C. Walthew
Lt. Col. O.F.C.
H.Q. 108 O.F.A.

WAR DIARY
or
INTELLIGENCE SUMMARY.

Hd. Qrs. 108 Bde. R.F.A.   Ref. Sheet 36 B.S.E. & C.S.W.

Army Form C. 2118.

Oct 16

Place	Date 1916	Hour	Summary of Events and Information	Remarks and references to Appendices
	Dec.			
VILLERS au BOIS	2/3		First portion of Battery relieved by 11th Bde R.F.A. LAHORE D.A. Borkun them relieved marched to billets at NOEUX-LES-MINES.	Elias
"	3/4		Remainder of Battery & Hd. Qrs. relieved by 11th Bde. R.F.A. & to billets at NOEUX-LES-MINES.	sent
NOEUX les MINES	4/5		First portion of Battery moved up into action in relief of 188 Bde R.F.A. 40th Div.	sent
LES BOEUFS			Remainder of Battery & Hd. Qrs. moved up into action. 2 Guns Bright from 24th Div.	
"			Supporting 73rd Infy Bde. in LOOS Sector. H.Qrs. at LES BOEUFS L.35.a 40.21.	
"			A Battery. G.33.a 44.70. 4 guns in L.19.c.66. B Battery. G.32.C 15.15. W.L. L.25.a.6.9.	
"			C Battery (two 18 gun in left group) G.32.d. 26.0.8. W.L. L.2d.a.5.2. D Battery. M.2d.15.85.	
"			W.L. L.31.a.4.4. C 106 (4 guns) attached. G.26 C.2.5.30.	sent
"	6		Lieut. C.D.D SWAIN posted to 186 Siege battery & struck off strength	sent
"	14		Lieut J ELLIOTT Joined & attached to A.	sent
"	27		Major C.E.B. DENNIS Joined & assumed command of A battery (from England)	sent
"	28		2/Lieut J.H. RIDGEWELL Joined on promotion from ranks. 40th Div.	sent

P.I. Whitehall
Lt. Col. R.F.A.
Cmdg 108 Bde. R.F.A.

www.ingramcontent.com/pod-product-compliance
Lightning Source LLC
Chambersburg PA
CBHW081545160426
43191CB00011B/1845